W9-BVG-871

FOOLPROOF CHINESE COOKING

KEN HOM

FOOLPROOF CHINESE COOKING

KEN HOM

Step by step to
everyone's favorite
Chinese recipes

London, New York, Sydney, Dehli, Paris,
Munich, and Johannesburg

Publisher: Sean Moore
Editorial director: LaVonne Carlson
Project editor: Barbara Minton
Editor: Jane Perlmutter
Jacket design: Gus Yoo
Production director: David Proffit

First US edition published in 2001 by
Dorling Kindersley Publishing, Inc.
95 Madison Avenue
New York, New York 10016

This is a companion book to the PBS Television series Great Food
Presented by
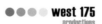
Sponsored by

www.looksmart.com
Produced by
west 175
productions
wine.com
The best of wine

First published by BBC Worldwide Ltd,
Woodlands, 80 Wood Lane,
London W12 0TT

First published 2000
Copyright © Promo Group Ltd 2000

Commissioning editor: Vivien Bowler
Project editor: Lara Speicher
Copy editor: Jane Middleton
Art direction: Lisa Pettibone
Designers: Norma Martin and Lisa Pettibone
Home economist: Linda Tubby
Stylist: Sue Rowlands
Food photography © Jean Cazals 2000

Library of Congress Cataloguing-in-Publication Data

Hom, Ken.
Foolproof Chinese cooking: step by step to everyone's favorite Chjinese recipes/ Ken Hom.
p. cm.
Includes index.
ISBN 0-7894-7145-0 (alk. paper)
1. Cookery, Chinese. I. Title.
TX724.5.C5 H65 2001
641.5951—dc21   00-058932

Set in Univers; Printed and bound in Singapore by Tien Wah Press
Color separations by Kestrel Digital Color, Chelmsford; Printed paper case and jacket by Tien Wah Press

Contents

Introduction 7

Ingredients and Equipment 8

Soups and First Courses 24
Classic Chinese chicken stock 26
Cantonese egg flower soup 28
Corn and crab soup 30
Cantonese wonton soup 32
Spicy hot and sour soup 34
Crispy "seaweed" 36
Sesame shrimp toast 38
Crispy fried wontons 40
Dim sum-style pork dumplings 42
Peking-style caramel walnuts 44
Spring rolls 46

Fish and Shellfish 50
Steamed Cantonese-style fish 52
Sichuan braised fish 54
Sweet and sour shrimp 56
Spicy Sichuan-style shrimp 58
Stir-fried squid with vegetables 60
Cantonese crab with
  black bean sauce 62
Steamed fresh oysters 66

Meat and Poultry 68
Stir-fried pork with spring onions 70
Sweet and sour pork,
  Chiu Chow style 72

Crackling Chinese roast pork 76
Stir-fried beef with
  oyster sauce 78
Stir-fried chicken with
  black bean sauce 80
Spicy chicken with peanuts 82
Classic lemon chicken 84
Chinese chicken curry 86
Cashew chicken 88
Peking duck 90
Crispy aromatic duck 92

Vegetables and
Side Dishes 94
Stir-fried spinach 96
Stir-fried broccoli 98
Stir-fried mixed vegetables 100
Braised Sichuan-style
  spicy beancurd 102
Sichuan-style green beans 104
Chinese pancakes 106
Perfect steamed rice 110
Egg-fried rice 112
Chow mein 114
Northern-style cold noodles 118
Singapore noodles 120

Menus 122

Index 127

Introduction

My knowledge and love of Chinese cooking came from watching and imitating chefs at my uncle's restaurant, where I was a young apprentice. Later, as a culinary professor, I was struck by the fact that, although many of my students had read about various techniques in one or more of the many fine Chinese cookbooks available, it was only when they saw them demonstrated that they really understood them. And only then could they attempt to duplicate what I had shown them. The step-by-step procedures that I developed became the basis of my teaching and I used them extensively as a broadcaster. They form the backbone of the recipes in this book. The cliché about pictures being worth a thousand words is more valid than ever.

China has one of the world's oldest culinary traditions. Its cuisine is unique because it developed independently of the West. Because of the ancient, insular civilization, poor transportation network, lack of arable land, shortage of fuels, and lack of ovens, Chinese chefs were forced to accommodate their art to necessity. Later, as the Chinese moved abroad, they took this culinary heritage with them. If one wishes to understand the essence of Chinese cooking, therefore, it is important to make a cultural leap of faith.

Chinese cooks are engaged in creating harmony. The size and shape of the food, the fragrances and the contrasting tastes and textures are all part of the final result. Our aim is to attain a balance among all these elements. Often when I demonstrate, people are surprised by the simplicity and logic of this ancient cuisine. The tools we use are remarkably few and simple and the techniques so effective that cooks from other cuisines now use many of them.

In this book, you will see that Chinese cooking is really not very complex. The step-by-step photographs and the thoroughly tested recipes will help you to achieve success. However, you should be bold. Trust your palate. Follow the techniques and recipes but feel free to add your own touches. Adjust and invent, as Chinese cooks have done for centuries. Incorporate your favorite Chinese ingredients when cooking dishes from other cuisines. Use the techniques that you have mastered from this book and build upon them.

It is my hope that the pleasure you gain from making these fool-proof recipes will give you the confidence of a true Chinese cook.

> "Chinese cooks are engaged in creating harmony. The size and shape of the food, the fragrances and the contrasting tastes and textures are all part of the final result."

Ingredients and Equipment

INGREDIENTS

Events of the past few decades have opened up the kitchens of the world to Asian food, and many of the most exotic ingredients are now readily available in the West. This is especially true of Chinese food. The following is a brief guide to ingredients used in this book.

Beancurd

Beancurd, also known by its Chinese name, *doufu*, or the Japanese, *tofu*, is highly nutritious and rich in protein with a distinctive texture and a bland taste. It is made from yellow soy beans, which are soaked, ground, mixed with water, and cooked briefly before being solidified. Beancurd is readily available in two forms – as firm cakes or as a thick-textured cream – and may also be found in several dried forms and in a fermented version. The soft cream-like variety (sometimes called silken tofu) is used for soups, and the solid type for stir-frying, braising, and poaching. Beancurd cakes are white in color and available in supermarkets and Asian markets, as well as in many health food stores. They are packed in water in plastic containers and may be kept in this state in the refrigerator for up to five days if the water is changed daily.

To use solid beancurd, cut it carefully into cubes or shreds with a sharp knife. It also needs to be cooked carefully, since too much stirring can cause it to crumble.

Bok Choy
(Chinese White Cabbage)

Although there are many varieties, the most common bok choy has long, smooth, milky-white stems and large, crinkly, dark green leaves. The smaller the plant, the more tender it will be. Bok choy has a light, fresh, slightly mustardy flavor and requires little cooking. It is now widely available in supermarkets. Look for firm, crisp stalks and unblemished leaves. Store bok choy in the vegetable crisper of your refrigerator.

Caul Fat

Caul fat is a lacy membrane that lines the stomach cavity of pigs and cows. It melts during cooking and is often used by European and Chinese cooks to encase stuffings and keep meat moist and delicious. You should be able to order caul fat from your butcher. It is highly perishable, so buy it in small quantities and use quickly. For longer storage, wrap the caul fat carefully and freeze it. To defrost, rinse in cold water. I find that soaking caul fat in cold water before use helps to separate the fat without tearing its lacy, fragile webs.

Chilies

Chilies are used extensively in western China, less so in the south. They are the seed pods of capsicum plants and can be obtained fresh, dried, or ground. There are many types available and they vary greatly in flavor and heat.

Fresh Chilies

Fresh chilies should look bright and shiny with no brown patches or black spots. As a general rule, red chilies are milder than green ones because they sweeten as they ripen, but nevertheless some red chilies can be very hot and spicy indeed.

To prepare fresh chilies, rinse them in cold water, then slit them lengthwise with a small sharp knife. Remove and discard the seeds. Rinse the chilies again under cold running water and then prepare them according to the recipe. Wash your hands, knife, and chopping board before preparing other foods, being careful not to touch your eyes until you have washed your hands thoroughly.

Dried Red Chilies

The dried red chilies used in China are usually small, thin and about ½ in (1 cm) long. They are normally left whole or cut in half lengthwise with the seeds left in and used to season oil for stir-fried dishes, sauces, and braises.

The Chinese like to blacken them and leave them in the dish during cooking but, since they are extremely hot, you may prefer to remove them immediately after using them to flavor the cooking oil. They can be found in Asian markets as well as in most supermarkets and will keep indefinitely in a tightly covered jar. When eating out, most diners carefully move the blackened chilies to one side of their plate.

Chili Oil/Chili Dipping Sauce

Chili oil is sometimes used as a dipping condiment as well as a seasoning in China.
It varies in strength according to the chilies used. The Thai and Malaysian versions are especially hot, the Taiwanese and Chinese ones more subtle. Commercial oils are quite acceptable but the homemade version is best, so I have included a recipe below. Remember that chili oil is too intense to be used as the sole cooking oil, so combine it with milder oils. This recipe includes pepper and black beans for additional flavors so it can also be used as a dipping sauce.

Green and red fresh chilies; dried red chilies

⅔ cup (150 ml) peanut oil
2 tablespoons chopped dried red chilies
1 tablespoon unroasted Sichuan peppercorns
2 tablespoons whole salted black beans

Heat a wok over a high heat, then add the oil followed by all the rest of the ingredients. Cook over a low heat for about 10 minutes, then remove from the heat and let the mixture cool. Pour into a jar and leave for 2 days, then strain the oil. Store in a tightly sealed glass jar in a cool, dark place, where it will keep indefinitely.

Chili Powder

Chili powder is made from dried red chilies and is used in many spicy dishes. As with chilies in general, add it according to taste.

Chinese Flowering Cabbage

Chinese flowering cabbage, or choi sum, is part of the mustard green cabbage family. It has green leaves and may have small yellow flowers, which can be eaten along with the leaves and stems. In China this is one of the most popular leafy vegetables and makes a delicious stir-fry dish.

Clockwise from top left: pak choy, chinese flowering cabbage, cilantro, bok choy

Chinese Leaves (Peking Cabbage)

This delicious, crunchy vegetable comes in various sizes, from long, compact, barrel-shaped ones to short, squat types. The heads are tightly packed with firm, pale green, or in some cases slightly yellow, crinkled leaves. It is most commonly added to soups and meat stir-fries but its ability to absorb flavors and its pleasant taste and texture make it a favorite with chefs, who match it with rich foods. Store it as you would ordinary cabbage.

Cilantro (Chinese Parsley)

Cilantro is one of the relatively few herbs used in Chinese cooking. It looks like flat-leaf parsley but its pungent, musky, citrus-like flavor gives it a distinctive character that is unmistakable. Its delicate leaves are often used as a garnish, or they can be chopped and mixed into sauces and stuffings. Parsley can be substituted, but the taste will not be the same.

When buying cilantro, choose deep-green leaves; limp, yellowing leaves indicate age and should be avoided. To store cilantro, wash it in cold water, dry thoroughly (preferably in a salad spinner) and wrap in paper towels. Put it in the vegetable compartment of your refrigerator, where it should keep for several days.

Cornstarch

In China there are many flours and types of starch, such as water chestnut powder, taro starch, and arrowroot. They are primarily used to bind ingredients together, thicken sauces, and make batters. These exotic starches and flours are difficult to obtain outside China but I have found that cornstarch works just as well in my recipes. Used in marinades, it helps to coat the food properly and it gives dishes a velvety texture. It also protects food during deep-frying by helping to seal in the juices, and can be used as a binder in ground stuffings. Before adding cornstarch to sauces, blend it to a smooth paste with a little cold water. During cooking, the cornstarch paste will turn clear and shiny.

Egg White

In Chinese recipes, egg whites are often used in batters and as a coating to seal in the food's flavor and juices when it is plunged into hot oil. It is especially important in velveting – a technique where chicken is coated in egg white and cornstarch, then blanched in oil or water. One large egg white is about 2 tablespoons. You can easily freeze raw egg whites in tablespoon-size cubes in an ice cube tray.

Five-spice Powder

Also known as five-flavored powder or five-fragrance spice powder, this is becoming a staple in the spice section of supermarkets, and Asian markets always keep it in stock. It is a mixture of ground star anise, Sichuan peppercorns, fennel, cloves, and cinnamon. A good blend will be pungent, fragrant, spicy, and slightly sweet. The exotic fragrance it gives to a dish makes the search for good five-spice powder well worth the effort. It keeps indefinitely in a tightly sealed jar.

Garlic

Garlic has been an essential seasoning in Chinese cooking for thousands of years. Indeed, Chinese food would be unrecognizable without its highly aromatic smell and distinctive taste. It is used to flavor oils as well as spicy sauces and is often paired with other

Garlic and ginger

pungent ingredients, such as scallions, black beans, and fresh ginger.

Select bulbs of garlic that are firm and preferably pinkish in color. Store in a cool, dry place but not in the refrigerator, where it can easily become mildewed or start sprouting.

Ginger

Fresh ginger is an indispensable ingredient in Chinese cooking. Its pungent, spicy taste adds a subtle but distinctive flavor to soups, meats and vegetables and it is also an important seasoning for fish and seafood, since it neutralizes fishy smells.

Ginger looks rather like a gnarled Jerusalem artichoke and can vary in length from 3–6 in (7.5–15 cm). Select firm, unshrivelled pieces and peel off the skin before use. It will keep in the refrigerator, well wrapped in plastic wrap, for about two weeks. Dried powdered ginger has a quite different flavor and should not be substituted for fresh.

Most of the recipes in this book that require ginger specify that it should be finely shredded or chopped. For shredded ginger, thinly slice a piece lengthwise, then stack and cut lengthwise again into fine strips. To chop finely, turn the shredded ginger around and chop it horizontally.

Ham

Chinese ham has a rich, salty flavor and is used primarily as a garnish or seasoning for soups, sauces, stir-fries, noodles, and rice. Prosciutto or lean smoked bacon (with any rind or fat cut away) makes a good substitute.

Snow Peas

This familiar vegetable combines a tender, crunchy texture with a sweet, fresh flavor. Look for firm pods with very small peas, which indicates they are tender and young. Snow peas should keep for about a week in the vegetable crisper of the refrigerator.

Mushrooms

Chinese Dried Mushrooms

There are many varieties of these, either black or brown, but the very large, pale ones with a cracked surface are the best. They are usually the most expensive, so use them sparingly. They are available in plastic packages or, in

Clockwise from top left: straw mushrooms, tree fungus, Chinese dried mushrooms, wood ear fungus

some Asian markets, they can be bought in bulk. Store in an airtight jar.

To use dried mushrooms, soak them in a bowl of warm water for about 20 minutes or until they are soft and pliable. Squeeze out the excess water, then cut off and discard the woody stems. Only the caps should be used. The soaking water can be saved and used in soups or for cooking rice. Strain it through a fine sieve to discard any sand or residue from the dried mushrooms.

Chinese Tree Fungus

These tiny, black, dried leaves are also known as cloud ears, because when soaked they puff up like little clouds. They are valued for their crunchy texture and slightly smoky flavor. You should be able to find them in Asian markets, usually wrapped in plastic bags. They keep indefinitely in a jar stored in a cool, dry place. Before use, soak them in hot water for 20–30 minutes until soft, then rinse well, cutting away any hard bits.

Chinese Wood Ear Fungus

This is a larger variety of the Chinese tree fungus described on the previous page. Soak and trim them in the same way before use. During soaking, they will swell up to four or five times their original size. They keep indefinitely when stored in a jar in a cool dry place.

Straw Mushrooms

These are among the most flavorful mushrooms found in China. When fresh they have deep brown caps which are molded around the stem. In the West they are only available in cans, from Asian markets, some supermarkets, and gourmet food shops. Drain and rinse in cold water before use.

Noodles

In China, people eat noodles (pasta) of all kinds, day and night, in restaurants and at food stalls. They provide a nutritious, quick, light snack and are usually of good quality. Several types of Chinese noodles have now made their way into the West.

Clockwise from top left: flat wheat noodles, beanthread noodles, egg noodles, rice noodles, round wheat noodles

Bean Thread (Transparent) Noodles

Also called cellophane noodles, these very fine, white noodles are made from ground mung beans. They are available dried, packed in neat, plastic-wrapped bundles, from Asian markets and supermarkets.

Bean thread noodles are never served on their own but are added to soups or braises or deep-fried and used as a garnish. Soak them in warm water for about 5 minutes before use. Since they are rather long, you might find it easier to cut them into shorter lengths after soaking. If you are frying them, they do not need soaking beforehand but they do need to be separated. The best way to do this is to pull them apart in a large paper bag, which stops them flying all over the place.

Rice Noodles

These dried noodles are opaque white and come in a variety of shapes and thicknesses. One of the most common is rice stick noodles, which are flat and about the length of a chopstick. Rice noodles are very easy to prepare. Simply soak them in warm water for 20 minutes until they are soft, then drain in a colander. They are now ready to be used in soups or stir-fried.

Wheat Noodles and Egg Noodles

Available dried or fresh, these are made from hard or soft wheat flour, water, and sometimes egg, in which case they are labeled egg noodles. Flat noodles are usually used in soups, while rounded ones are best for frying. The fresh ones freeze well if they are tightly wrapped. Thaw thoroughly before cooking.

Dried wheat or fresh egg noodles are very good blanched and served as an accompaniment to main dishes instead of plain rice. If you are cooking noodles ahead of time or before stir-frying them, toss the cooked, drained noodles in 2 teaspoons of sesame oil and put them into a bowl. Cover this with plastic wrap and refrigerate for up to 2 hours.

Oils

Oil is the most commonly used cooking medium in China, although animal fats, usually lard and chicken fat, are also used in some areas, particularly in the north.

To re-use oil after deep-frying, let it cool, then filter it through muslin or a fine sieve into a jar. Seal and store in a cool, dry place. If you keep it in the refrigerator, it will become cloudy, but it clarifys again when it returns to room temperature. Oils are best re-used only once, which is healthier because their saturated fat content increases the more you use them.

Peanut Oil

I prefer to use peanut oil for Chinese cooking because it has a pleasant, unobtrusive taste. Although it has a higher saturated fat content than some oils, its ability to be heated to a high temperature without burning makes it perfect for stir-frying and deep-frying. Most supermarkets stock peanut oil but if you cannot find it, use corn oil instead.

Corn Oil

Corn oil is also quite suitable for Chinese cooking, since it has a high heating point. However, I find it rather bland and with a slightly disagreeable smell. It is high in polyunsaturates and is therefore one of the healthier oils.

Other Vegetable Oils

Some of the cheaper vegetable oils available include soy bean, safflower, and sunflower. Light in color and taste, they can be used in Chinese cooking but take care, since they smoke and burn at lower temperatures than peanut oil.

Sesame Oil

This thick, rich, golden-brown oil made from sesame seeds has a distinctive, nutty flavor and aroma. It is widely used in Chinese cooking as a seasoning but is not normally used as a cooking oil because it burns easily. Think of it more as a flavoring than a cooking oil. A small amount is often added at the last moment to finish a dish.

Peanuts

Raw peanuts are widely used in Chinese cooking to add flavor and crunch. They are especially good when marinated or added to stir-fry dishes. The thin red skins should be removed before use. To do this, simply immerse the nuts in a pan of boiling water for about 2 minutes, then drain and let them cool; the skins will come off easily.

Shrimp

For most of the recipes in this book you will need medium to large raw, unshelled shrimp. These are sweeter and more succulent than ready-cooked ones. Before cooking, they should be shelled and, if large, deveined. To remove the shell, twist off the head and discard, then, using your fingers, break open the shell along the belly and peel it off. Run a small, sharp knife along the back of the shrimp and pull out the dark intestinal vein. The tail shell can be left on for presentation.

Rice

There are many different varieties of rice in China but long grain is the most popular. Although the Chinese go through the ritual of washing it, rice purchased at supermarkets doesn't require this step. However, if you wish to do as the Chinese do, put the rice into a large bowl, fill it with cold water and swish the rice around with your hands. Carefully pour off the cloudy water, keeping the rice in the bowl. Repeat this process several times until the water is clear.

Tiger shrimp

Clockwise from top: chili bean sauce, hoisin sauce, yellow bean sauce, oyster sauce, chili oil

Salt

Table salt is the finest grind but many cooks believe that the coarser sea salt has a richer flavor. Sea salt is frequently sold in bulk at Asian markets. Rock salt is often used in certain kinds of *chaozhou* (a cooking style from southern China), especially with chicken dishes.

Salted Black Beans

These small black soy beans are fermented with salt and spices to preserve them. Their distinctive flavor makes them a tasty seasoning, especially when used with garlic or fresh ginger. They are inexpensive and can be bought at Asian markets, usually in cans labeled "black beans in salted sauce," but you may also see them packed in plastic bags. Rinse them before use as an optional step; I prefer to chop them slightly, too, to release their pungent flavor. Transfer any unused beans and liquid to a sealed jar and they will keep indefinitely in the refrigerator. For convenience, brands of black bean sauce are now available in supermarkets, which in many cases are authentic and quite acceptable.

Sauces and Pastes

Chinese and Asian cooking involves a number of tasty sauces and pastes. They are essential for authentic Chinese cooking, and it is well worth making the effort to obtain them. Most are sold in jars or cans by Asian markets and some supermarkets. Once opened, canned sauces should be transferred to screw-top glass jars and kept in the refrigerator, where they will last indefinitely.

Chili Bean Sauce

This thick, dark sauce or paste is made from soy beans, chilies, and other seasonings, and is very hot and spicy. Be sure to seal the jar tightly after use and store in the cupboard or refrigerator. Do not confuse it with chili sauce (see below), which is a hotter, redder, thinner condiment made without beans.

Chili Sauce

This hot, bright red sauce, made from chilies, vinegar, sugar, and salt, is mainly used as a dipping sauce. There are various brands available in Asian markets and many supermarkets and you should experiment with them until you find the one you like best. If you find chili sauce too strong, dilute it with hot water. Do not confuse this sauce with chili bean sauce (see above), which is a much thicker, darker sauce used for cooking.

Hoisin Sauce

This thick, dark, brownish red sauce, made from soy beans, vinegar, sugar, spices, and other flavorings, is sweet and spicy. It is sold in cans and jars (it is sometimes also called barbecue sauce) and is available in Asian markets and supermarkets. If refrigerated, it should keep indefinitely.

Oyster Sauce

This thick, brown sauce is made from a concentrate of oysters cooked in soy sauce and brine. Despite its name, it does not taste fishy. It has a rich flavor and is used not only in cooking but also as a condiment, diluted with a little oil, for serving with vegetables, poultry, and meat dishes. It is usually sold in jars and can be bought in supermarkets and Asian markets. I find it keeps best in the refrigerator. A vegetarian oyster sauce made with mushrooms is now available.

Sesame Paste

This rich, thick, creamy, brown paste is made from sesame seeds and is used in both hot and cold dishes. If you cannot obtain it, use peanut butter, which has a similar texture. Don't substitute tahini, the Middle Eastern sesame seed paste, because the flavor is not as strong as the Asian paste.

Soy Sauce

Soy sauce is an essential ingredient in Chinese cooking. It is made from a mixture of soy beans, flour, and water, which is then fermented naturally and aged for some months. The liquid that is finally distilled is soy sauce.

There are two main types. Light soy sauce, as the name implies, is light in color but full of flavor and that makes it the better one to use for cooking. It is saltier than dark soy sauce, and is known in Asian markets as Superior Soy. Dark soy sauce, confusingly, is known as Soy Superior Sauce. It is aged for much longer than light soy sauce, hence its darker, almost black color, and it is also slightly thicker and stronger. It is more suitable for stews. I prefer it to light soy as a dipping sauce.

Supermarkets tend to sell dark soy sauce. Asian markets sell both types and the quality is excellent. Be sure you buy the correct one, since the names are very similar.

Whole Yellow Bean Sauce

This thick, spicy, aromatic sauce is made of yellow beans, flour, and salt, which are fermented together. It is quite salty, and adds a distinctive flavor to Chinese sauces. There are two forms: whole beans in a thick sauce, and mashed or puréed beans (sold as crushed yellow bean sauce). I prefer the whole bean variety because it is slightly less salty and has a better texture.

Sesame Seeds

These are the dried seeds of the sesame plant. Unhulled, the seeds range from grayish white to black in color. The tiny hulled seeds are cream colored and pointed at one end. Stored in a glass jar in a cool, dry place, they will last indefinitely.

To toast sesame seeds, heat a frying pan, then add the seeds and stir occasionally. Watch them closely to make sure they don't burn. When they begin to brown lightly, after about 3–5 minutes, stir them again and turn them out onto a plate. Allow to cool, then store in a glass jar in a cool, dark place.

Alternatively, you could spread the sesame seeds on a baking sheet and roast them in an oven preheated to 325°F/160°C for 10–15 minutes, until lightly browned.

Shaoxing Rice Wine

Rice wine is used extensively for cooking and drinking throughout China, but I believe the finest of its many varieties to be from Shaoxing in Zhejiang Province in Eastern China. It is made from glutinous rice, yeast, and spring water. Now readily available in Asian markets and in some wine shops in the West, it should be kept tightly corked at room temperature. A good quality, pale dry sherry can be substituted but cannot match the rice wine's rich, mellow taste. Do not confuse this wine with sake, which is the Japanese version of rice wine and quite different. Western grape wines are not an adequate substitute either.

Sherry

If you cannot get rice wine, use a good quality, dry pale sherry instead. Do not use sweet or cream sherries.

Sichuan Peppercorns

Sichuan peppercorns are known throughout China as "flower peppers" because they look like flower buds opening. They are reddish brown, with a strong, pungent odor that distinguishes them from the hotter black peppercorns. They are actually not from peppers at all; instead they are the dried berries of a shrub belonging to the citrus family. Their smell reminds me of lavender but their taste is sharp and mildly spicy.

Sichuan peppercorns are inexpensive and will keep indefinitely if stored in a well-sealed container. They can be ground in a conventional peppermill and are very often roasted first to bring out the full flavor. To roast them, heat a wok or heavy frying-pan to a medium heat. Add the peppercorns, cooking about 5 oz (150 g) at a time, and stir-fry them for about 5 minutes until they brown slightly and start to smoke. Remove the pan from the heat and let them cool. Grind the peppercorns in a peppermill, a clean coffee grinder, or with a mortar and pestle. Store in a tightly sealed screw-top

scallions (from top) finely chopped, shredded, cut on the round, cut on the diagonal

jar. Alternatively keep the whole roasted peppercorns in a well-sealed container and grind them when required.

Spinach

Western varieties of spinach are quite different from those used in China, but they make satisfactory substitutes. Spinach is most commonly stir-fried, so frozen spinach is unsuitable since it is so moist. Chinese water spinach is the most common type in China and is sometimes available in Asian markets in the West. It has hollow stems, delicate, pointed, green leaves, and a paler color and milder flavor than common spinach. It should be cooked when very fresh, preferably on the day you purchase it.

Scallions

The recipes in this book specify a variety of ways to prepare scallions, both for cooking and for garnish. First, peel off the outer layer if it is bruised or damaged. Trim the tops and bottom and remove any damaged green tops.

To chop finely, split into quarters lengthways, then chop into small pieces horizontally. To shred, cut the onions in half horizontally, then split very finely lengthwise. To curl shredded scallions, put them in a bowl of ice-cold water. This makes an attractive garnish. scallions can also be cut simply on the round at various thicknesses, and also on the diagonal, which is useful for certain recipes and also looks pretty as a garnish.

Spring Roll Skins

These 6 in (15 cm) square, paper-thin wrappers are made from a soft flour and water dough. They are available in packages of 20 from Asian markets and keep well in the freezer if wrapped in plastic wrap.

Star Anise

Star anise is a hard, star-shaped spice, the seed pod of an attractive bush. It is similar in flavor and fragrance to common anise but more robust and liquorice-like. Star anise is an essential ingredient in five-spice powder (see page 10) and is widely used in braised dishes, to which it imparts a rich taste and fragrance. It is available in plastic packages from Asian markets and should be stored in a sealed jar in a cool, dry place.

Sugar

Used sparingly, sugar helps to balance the flavors of sauces and other dishes. Chinese sugar comes in several forms: as rock or yellow lump sugar, as brown sugar slabs, and as maltose or malt sugar. I particularly like to use rock sugar, which has a richer, more subtle flavor than refined granulated sugar and gives a good luster to braised dishes and sauces. It is available in packets from Asian markets. You may need to break the lumps into smaller pieces with a wooden mallet or rolling pin. If you cannot find it, use white sugar or turbinato sugar (the amber, chunky kind) instead.

Vinegar

Vinegars are widely used in Chinese cooking. Unlike Western vinegars, they are usually made from rice. There are many varieties, ranging in flavor from spicy to slightly tart to sweet and pungent. They can be bought in Asian markets and keep indefinitely. If you cannot get Chinese vinegar, use cider vinegar. Malt vinegar can be substituted if necessary but its taste is stronger and more acidic.

White Rice Vinegar
This clear vinegar has a mild flavor with a faint taste of glutinous rice. It is used in sweet and sour dishes.

Black Rice Vinegar
Black rice vinegar is very dark in color and rich, though mild, in taste. It is used for braised dishes, sauces, and sometimes as a dipping sauce for crab.

Red Rice Vinegar
This is sweet and spicy, and is normally used as a dipping sauce for seafood.

Water Chestnuts

Water chestnuts are a white, sweet, crunchy bulb about the size of a walnut. In China they are often simmered in rock sugar and eaten as a snack. They are also used in cooked dishes, especially in southern China.

In the West, canned water chestnuts are sold in many supermarkets and Asian markets. They have a good texture but little taste. Rinse them well in cold water before use and store any unused ones in a jar of cold water. They will keep for several weeks in the refrigerator

Clockwise from top: fresh water chestnuts, star anise, Sichuan peppercorns, wonton skins

if you change the water daily. Fresh water chestnuts can sometimes be obtained from Asian markets or good supermarkets. They are tastier than canned ones and will keep, unpeeled, in a paper bag in the refrigerator for up to 2 weeks. Peel them before use and put any leftover ones back in the refrigerator, covered with cold water.

Wonton Skins

These thin, yellowish, pastry-like wrappings made from egg and flour can be stuffed with ground meat and fried, steamed, or used in soups. They are available fresh or frozen from Asian markets or supermarkets, sold in little piles of 3¼ in (8 cm) squares, wrapped in plastic. Fresh wonton skins will keep for about 5 days in the refrigerator if wrapped in plastic wrap or a plastic bag. If you are using frozen wonton skins, just peel off the number you require and let thaw them completely.

EQUIPMENT

Traditional cooking equipment is not essential for the preparation of Chinese food but in some cases will make it very much easier. These implements have been tested through many centuries of use. Once you become familiar with woks and clay pots, for example, you will have entered the culinary world of China.

Wok

All your faith in Chinese cooking and your own skills will come to nothing without a good wok. This versatile piece of equipment can be used not only for stir-frying but also for blanching, deep-frying, and steaming. Its shape permits fuel-efficient, quick-and-even heating and cooking. When stir-frying, the deep sides prevent the food from spilling over; when deep-frying, much less oil is required because of the tapered base of the wok.

There are two basic types: the traditional Cantonese version, with short, rounded handles on either side, and the *pau*, sometimes called the Peking wok, which has one 12–14 in (30–35 cm) long handle. The long-handled wok keeps you at a safer distance from the possibility of splashing hot oil or water.

The standard round-bottomed wok may only be used on gas burners. Ones with flatter bottoms are now available, designed especially for electric burners. Although this shape really defeats the purpose of the traditional design, which is to concentrate intense heat at the center, it is better than an ordinary frying-pan because it has deeper sides.

Choosing a Wok

Choose a large wok – preferably about 12–14 in (30–35 cm) in diameter, with deep sides. It is easier and safer to cook a small batch of food in a large wok than a large quantity in a small one. Be aware that some modernized woks are too shallow or too flat-bottomed and thus no better than a frying-pan. A heavier wok, preferably made of carbon steel, is superior to the lighter stainless steel or aluminum type, which cannot take very high heat and tends to blacken as well as scorch the food. Good non-stick carbon steel woks that maintain the heat without sticking are now on the market. They need special care to prevent scratching, but in recent years the non-stick technology has improved, so that they can now be safely recommended. They are especially useful when cooking food that has a high acid level, such as lemons.

Seasoning a Wok

All woks except non-stick ones should be seasoned before first use. Many need to be scrubbed as well to remove the machine oil that is applied to the surface by the manufacturer to protect it in transit. This is the only time you will ever need to scrub your wok – unless you let it become rusty.

Scrub it with a non-abrasive cleanser and water to remove as much of the machine oil as possible. Then dry it and put it on the burner over a low heat. Add 2 tablespoons of cooking oil, and using paper towels, rub the oil over the inside of the wok until the entire surface is lightly coated. Heat the wok slowly for about 10–15 minutes and then wipe it thoroughly with more paper towels. The paper will become blackened. Repeat this process of coating, heating, and wiping until the paper towel no longer colors. With use, your wok will darken and become well seasoned, which is a good sign.

Cleaning a Wok

Once your wok has been seasoned, you should never scrub it with soap or water. Just wash it in plain clear water and dry it thoroughly after each use – putting the cleaned wok over a low heat for a minute or two should do the trick. If it does rust a bit, scrub it with a non-abrasive cleanser and re-season.

Stir-frying in a Wok

The most important thing when stir-frying is to have all your ingredients ready to use – this is a very fast method of cooking and you will not have time to stop and chop things while you are cooking.

Heat the wok until it is very hot, then add the oil and distribute it evenly over the surface using a metal spatula or long-handled spoon. The oil should be very hot – almost smoking – before you add the ingredients.

Add the food to be cooked and stir-fry by tossing it around the wok or pan with a metal spatula or long-handled spoon. If you are stir-frying meat, let each side rest for a few seconds before continuing to stir. Keep moving the food from the center of the wok to the sides.

I prefer to use a long-handled wok, since there can be a lot of splattering due to the high temperature at which the food must be cooked.

Wok Accessories

Wok Stand
This is a metal ring or frame designed to keep a conventionally shaped wok steady on the burner. It is essential if you want to use your wok for steaming, deep-frying, or braising. Stands come in two designs: a solid metal ring punched with about six ventilation holes, and a circular, thin wire frame. If you have a gas stove use only the latter type, since the more solid design does not allow for sufficient ventilation and may lead to a build-up of gas, which could put the flame out completely.

Wok Lid
This light, inexpensive domed cover, usually made from aluminum, is used for steaming. It is normally supplied with the wok, but if not, may be purchased at a Chinese or Asian market, or you may use any domed saucepan lid that fits snugly.

Spatula
A long-handled metal spatula shaped rather like a small shovel is ideal for scooping and tossing food in a wok. Alternatively any good long-handled spoon can be used.

Rack
When steaming food in your wok, you will need a wooden or metal rack or trivet to raise the food above the water level. Wok sets usually include a rack but, if not, Asian markets sell them separately. Department and hardware stores also sell wooden and metal stands which can serve the same purpose. Any rack, improvised or not, that keeps the food above the water, so that it is steamed and not boiled, will suffice.

Bamboo Brush
This bundle of stiff, split bamboo is used for cleaning a wok without scrubbing off the seasoned surface. It is an attractive, inexpensive implement but not essential. A soft dishwashing sponge will do just as well.

Chopping Board
One decided improvement over traditional Chinese cooking implements is the modern chopping board made of hardwood or acrylic. Typical Chinese chopping boards are made of soft wood, which is difficult to maintain and, being soft, provides a fertile surface for bacteria. Hardwood or acrylic boards are easy to clean, resist bacterial accumulation, and last much longer. Chinese cooking entails much chopping, slicing, and dicing so it is essential to have a large, steady chopping board. For hygienic reasons, never place ready to serve food on a board on which raw meat or poultry has been prepared. For raw meat, always use a separate board and clean it thoroughly after each use.

Chopsticks
Many Western diners feel challenged by chopsticks, but I always encourage their use. Attempting any new technique is an interesting experience, and chopsticks do indeed offer the novice a physical entrée into Chinese cuisine. They are used as a combination spoon and fork, and for stirring, beating, whipping, and mixing. But, of course, you can also get along nicely with Western spoons, forks, ladles, spatulas, and whisks.

Chopsticks are cheap and readily available. I prefer the wooden ones but in China plastic ones are more commonly used (and reused) for economic reasons.

Cleaver
To Chinese cooks, the cleaver is an all-purpose cutting instrument that makes all other knives redundant. Once you acquire some skill with a cleaver you will see how it can be used for all types of food to slice, dice, chop, fillet, shred, crush, or whatever. In practice, most Chinese chefs rely upon three different sizes of cleaver – light, medium, and heavy – to be used appropriately. Of course, you may use your own familiar kitchen knives instead, but if you decide to invest in a cleaver choose a good quality stainless steel model and make sure to keep it sharpened.

Wok with lid, spatula, chopsticks, wok stand, cleaver, and rack

Deep-fat Fryer

A deep-fat fryer is very useful and you may find it safer and easier to use for deep-frying than a wok. The quantities of oil given in the recipes in this book are based on the amount required for deep-frying in a wok. If you are using a deep-fat fryer instead, you will need about double that amount, but never fill the fryer more than half-full with oil.

Rice Cooker

Electric rice cookers are increasingly popular. They cook rice perfectly and keep it warm throughout the meal. They also have the advantage of freeing a burner or element so the stovetop is less cluttered. They are relatively expensive, however, so are only worth buying if you eat rice frequently.

Clay or Sand Pots

The Chinese rely upon these lightweight clay pots for braised dishes, soups, and rice cooking. Their unglazed exteriors have a sandy texture, hence their name, and their design allows the infusion of aromas and tastes into foods. Clay pots are available in many sizes, with matching lids, and being quite fragile, they are often encased in a wire frame. They should be used directly on the burner (most Chinese do not have ovens) but never put an empty clay pot on a heated element or a hot clay pot on a cold surface: the shock will crack it. Clay pots should always have at least some liquid in them, and when filled with food, they can take very high heat. If you have an electric stove, use an asbestos pad to insulate the pot from direct contact with the hot coils. Note that because of the release of hot steam you should always lift the lid away from you.

Steamer

Steaming is not a very popular cooking method in the West. This is unfortunate because it is the best way of preparing many foods with a delicate taste and texture, such as fish and vegetables. In China, bamboo steamers have been in use for thousands of years. They come in several sizes of which the 10 in (25 cm) one is the most suitable for home use. The food is placed in the steamer, which is then placed above boiling water in a wok or pot. To stop the food sticking to the steamer as it cooks, put it on a layer of clean, damp cheesecloth. A tight-fitting bamboo lid prevents the steam escaping; several steamers, stacked one above the other, may be used simultaneously.

Before using a bamboo steamer for the first time, wash it and then steam it with nothing in it for about 5 minutes. Of course, any kind of wide metal steamer may be used, instead, if you prefer.

Miscellaneous

Stainless steel bowls of different sizes, along with sieves and colanders, round out the list of basic implements. They are very useful because you will often have to drain or strain oils and juices and because you will be doing much mixing of wonderful foods. It is better to have one too many tools than one too few.

Clay pots and bamboo steamers

Conversion tables

Conversions are approximate and have been rounded up or down. Follow one set of measurements only – do not mix US (American Standard) and metric.

Weights		Volume		Measurements	
US	**Metric**	**US**	**Metric**	**US**	**Metric**
½ oz	15 g	1 teaspoon	5 ml	¼ inch	0.5 cm
1 oz	25 g	1 tablespoon	15 ml	½ inch	1 cm
1½ oz	40 g	½ oz (1 tablespoon)	15 ml	1 inch	2.5 cm
2 oz	50 g	1 fl oz	29 ml	2 inches	5 cm
3 oz	75 g	2 fl oz	58 ml	3 inches	7.5 cm
4 oz	100 g	3 fl oz	87 ml	4 inches	10 cm
5 oz	150 g	4 fl oz (½ cup)	125 ml	6 inches	15 cm
6 oz	175 g	5 fl oz (⅔ cup)	148 ml	7 inches	18 cm
7 oz	200 g	6 fl oz (¾ cup)	177 ml	8 inches	20 cm
8 oz	225 g	7 fl oz (⅞ cup)	175 ml	9 inches	23 cm
9 oz	250 g	8 fl oz (1 cup)	250 ml	10 inches	25 cm
10 oz	275 g	10 fl oz (1¼ cup)	300 ml	12 inches	30 cm
12 oz	350 g	14 fl oz (1¾ cup)	400 ml		
13 oz	375 g	16 fl oz (1 pint)	600 ml		

Oven temperatures	
275°F	140°C
300°F	150°C
325°F	160°C
350°F	180°C
375°F	190°C
400°F	200°C
425°F	220°C
450°F	230°C
475°F	240°C

Weights		Volume	
14 oz	400 g	20 fl oz (1½ pints)	590 ml
15 oz	425 g	32 fl oz (1 quart)	945 ml
1 lb	450 g	34 fl oz	1 liter
1¼ lb	550 g	50 fl oz	1.5 liters
1½ lb	675 g	67.6 fl oz	2 liters
2 lb	900 g	109 fl oz	3 liters
3 lb	1.5 kg	128 fl oz (4 quarts)	3.75 liters
4 lb	1.75 kg	4 quarts (1 gal)	3.75 liters
5 lb	2.25 kg	169 fl oz	5 liters

SOUPS and FIRST COURSES

Classic Chinese chicken stock

Your first step on the path to success with Chinese cooking is to prepare and maintain an ample supply of good chicken stock. I prefer to make a large amount and freeze it. Once you have a supply of stock available you will be able to prepare any number of soups or sauces very quickly.

makes about 14 cups (3.4 liters)
preparation time: 15 minutes
cooking time: 3–5 hours

Chicken stock is light, delicious and inexpensive to make. It marries well with other foods, enhancing and sustaining them. Small wonder that it is an almost universally present ingredient in Chinese cooking, from the Imperial kitchens to the most humble food stands. The usual Chinese chicken stock is very simple: the essence of chicken, with complements of ginger and scallion often added. Combined with the condiments that give Chinese food its distinctive flavor, good stock captures the essential taste of China. The simple recipe given here reflects what I believe works best for any Chinese dish. The classic Chinese method of guaranteeing a clear stock is to blanch the meat and bones before simmering. I find this unnecessary. My method of careful skimming achieves the same result with far less work.

Commercially prepared canned or dried stocks are available, but many of them are of inferior quality since they are either too salty or contain additives and colorings that can adversely affect

your health and the natural taste of good food. Stock takes time to prepare, but you can easily make your own – and homemade tastes the best. Here are several important points to keep in mind when making stock:

- Good stock requires meat to give it richness and flavor. It is therefore essential to use at least some chicken pieces, if not a whole bird.
- Use a tall, heavy pot so the liquid covers all the solids and evaporation is slow.
- The stock should never boil. If it does it will become cloudy and the fat will be incorporated into the liquid. Flavor and digestibility come with a clear stock.
- Simmer the stock slowly and skim it regularly. Be patient; you will reap the rewards each time you prepare a Chinese dish.
- Strain the finished stock through several layers of cheesecloth or a fine sieve.
- Allow the stock to cool thoroughly, then chill it, and remove the layer of hardened fat on the surface before freezing.

4½ lb (2 kg) raw chicken backs, wings, feet, etc, or any leftover bones you may have (save chicken bones and keep them in your freezer until you need them)

1½ lb (675 g) chicken pieces, such as wings, thighs, drumsticks

5 quarts (5 liters) cold water

3 slices of fresh ginger, cut into diagonal slices 2 x ½ in (5 x 1 cm)

6 scallions, green tops removed

6 garlic cloves, unpeeled but lightly crushed

1 teaspoon salt

1 Put all the chicken into a very large pot (the bones can be put in either frozen or defrosted). Cover with the cold water and bring to a simmer.

2 Using a large, shallow spoon, skim off the foam as it rises to the surface of the water from the bones. Watch the heat—the stock should never boil. Keep skimming, as necessary, until the stock becomes clear. This can take 20–40 minutes at a low simmer. Do not stir or disturb the stock.

3 Now add the ginger, scallions, garlic cloves, and salt. Simmer the stock on a very low heat for 2–4 hours, skimming fat from the top at least twice. The stock should be rich and full-bodied, which results when it has been simmered for a long time.

4 Strain the stock through layers of dampened cheesecloth or through a very fine sieve. Let it cool thoroughly, then chill. Remove any fat that has risen to the top. It is now ready to be used or transferred to containers and frozen for future use.

Cantonese egg flower soup

This easy soup is found in almost every Chinese restaurant. No wonder; it is tasty and fantastically exotic. Lightly beaten egg lies flat on the surface of the soup like lilies on a pond. This effect is created by gently guiding the egg over the soup in strands instead of dropping the mixture in all at once, which would cause it to lump together. The egg mixture slightly thickens the soup, which nonetheless remains very light. As with any good soup, the most important thing is the stock upon which it is based.

1 egg, lightly beaten

2 teaspoons sesame oil

9 cups (1.2 liters) *Classic Chinese chicken stock* (see page 26) or good quality ready-made stock

1 teaspoon sugar

1 teaspoon salt

1 tablespoon light soy sauce

3 tablespoons finely shredded scallions, white part only

3 tablespoons finely shredded green scallion tops, to garnish

serves 4
preparation time: 5 minutes
cooking time: 5 minutes

1 Put the egg and sesame oil in a small jug or bowl, mix with a fork and set aside.

2 Put the stock into a pot and bring to a simmer. Add the sugar, salt, and soy sauce and stir to mix them in well. Stir in the white part of the scallions.

3 Next add the egg mixture in a very slow, thin stream.

4 Using chopsticks or a fork, pull the egg slowly into strands. I find that stirring the egg in a figure of eight works quite well. Garnish with the green scallion tops.

Corn and crab soup

This popular Chinese soup has captivated Western diners. My mother often made it using fresh corn. For convenience, canned or frozen corn may be substituted but I think my mother's recipe is superior.

serves 4
preparation time: 5 minutes
cooking time: 10 minutes

1 lb (450 g) corn on the cob, or 10 oz (275 g) canned or frozen corn

1 egg white

1 teaspoon sesame oil

5 cups (1.2 liters) *Classic Chinese chicken stock* (see page 26) or good quality ready-made stock

1 tablespoon Shaoxing rice wine or dry sherry

1 tablespoon light soy sauce

2 teaspoons finely chopped fresh ginger

1 teaspoon salt

½ teaspoon freshly ground white pepper

1 teaspoon sugar

2 teaspoons cornstarch, blended with 2 teaspoons water

8 oz (225 g) fresh or frozen crabmeat

2 tablespoons finely chopped scallions, to garnish

1 If you are using fresh corn, pull back the husks, wash the cobs, and remove the kernels with a sharp knife or cleaver. You should end up with about 1½ cups (275 g) corn.

2 Mix the egg white and sesame oil together in a small bowl or measuring cup and set aside.

3 Bring the stock to a boil in a large pot and add the corn. Simmer for 5 minutes, uncovered, then add the rice wine or sherry, light soy sauce, ginger, salt, pepper, sugar, and the cornstarch mixture. Bring back to a boil, then lower the heat to a simmer. Add the crabmeat.

4 Immediately afterwards, slowly pour in the egg white mixture in a steady stream, stirring all the time. Transfer the soup to a tureen or individual bowls and garnish with the scallions.

Cantonese wonton soup

This is one of the most popular soups in food stands through-out southern China and it is equally popular in Chinese restaurants in the West. Soup wonton should be stuffed savory dumplings poached in clear water and then served in a rich broth. Unfortunately in many restaurants the soup arrives with wonton skins but very little filling. This recipe will enable you to make a simple but authentic wonton soup. Wonton skins can be obtained, fresh or frozen, from Asian markets.

8 oz (225 g) wonton skins, thawed if necessary

5 cups (1.2 liters) *Classic Chinese chicken stock* (see page 26) or good quality ready-made stock

1 tablespoon light soy sauce

1 teaspoon sesame oil

Chopped green scallion tops, to garnish

For the filling:

½ lb (225 g) raw shrimp, peeled, veined (see page 13) and coarsely chopped

½ lb (225 g) ground pork

1 teaspoon salt

½ teaspoon freshly ground black pepper

1½ tablespoons light soy sauce

3 tablespoons finely chopped scallions (white part only)

2 teaspoons finely chopped fresh ginger

1 tablespoon Shaoxing rice wine or dry sherry

1 teaspoon sugar

2 teaspoons sesame oil

1 egg white, lightly beaten

serves 4

preparation time: 30 minutes, plus at least 20 minutes' chilling

cooking time: 10 minutes

1 For the filling, put the shrimp and pork in a large bowl, add the salt and pepper, and mix well, either by kneading with your hand or stirring with a wooden spoon.

2 Add all the other filling ingredients and mix thoroughly. Cover the bowl with plastic wrap and chill for at least 20 minutes.

5 Remove the wontons immediately and transfer them to
the pot of stock. (Poaching
them first results in a cleaner-
tasting broth.) Simmer them
in the stock for 2 minutes.
Transfer to a soup tureen or
individual bowls, garnish
with the scallion tops and
serve immediately.

3 To stuff the wontons, put
1 tablespoon of the filling in
the center of each wonton
skin. Dampen the edges with
a little water and bring them
up around the filling. Pinch
the edges together at the top
so that the wonton is sealed;
it should look like a small,
filled bag.

4 Put the stock, soy sauce and
sesame oil in a large pot and
bring to a simmer. Mean-
while, bring a large pan of
salted water to a boil and
poach the wontons in it in
batches for 1 minute or until
they float to the top.

Spicy hot and sour soup

This northern and western Chinese soup has become quite popular in the Western world because it is a hearty dish, suited to cold climates. It combines sour and spicy elements in a rich, tasty stock and reheats very well. The list of ingredients may look daunting but in fact the soup is quite easy to make. Replete with contrasting textures and flavors, it makes an engaging alternative to Western style soups.

5 cups (1.2 liters) *Classic Chinese chicken stock* (see page 26) or good quality ready-made stock

2 teaspoons salt

¼ lb (100 g) lean pork, finely shredded

1 oz (25 g) Chinese dried mushrooms, soaked, stems removed (see page 11)

½ oz (15 g) dried tree mushrooms or wood ear mushrooms, soaked, stems removed (see page 11)

8 oz (225 g) fresh firm beancurd, drained

2 eggs, beaten with a pinch of salt

4 teaspoons sesame oil

1½ tablespoons light soy sauce

1 tablespoon dark soy sauce

1 teaspoon freshly ground white pepper

6 tablespoons Chinese white rice vinegar or cider vinegar

2 teaspoons chili oil

2 tablespoons finely chopped cilantro

For the marinade:

1 teaspoon light soy sauce

1 teaspoon Shaoxing rice wine or dry sherry

½ teaspoon sesame oil

½ teaspoon cornstarch

A pinch of salt

A pinch of sugar

serves 4
preparation time: 25 minutes
cooking time: 5 minutes

1 Bring the stock to a simmer in a large pot and add the salt. Meanwhile, combine the pork with the marinade ingredients, mix well, and set aside.

2 Finely shred the soaked mushrooms, tree or wood ear mushrooms, and beancurd and set aside. In a bowl, combine the eggs with 2 teaspoons of the sesame oil.

5 Remove the soup from the heat, and add the soy sauces, white pepper, and vinegar. Give the soup a good stir, then stir in the remaining sesame oil, plus the chili oil and cilantro. Ladle into a soup tureen or individual bowls and serve.

3 Stir the pork into the stock and simmer for 1 minute. Then add the mushrooms and beancurd and simmer for another 2 minutes.

4 Pour in the egg mixture in a slow, thin, steady stream. Using chopsticks or a fork, pull the egg slowly into strands.

Crispy "seaweed"

This is one of the most popular Chinese restaurant dishes in the West. A special type of seaweed is used in China, but it is not yet available elsewhere so Chinese cabbage is used instead. This is a good example of the adaptability of Chinese cuisine: if the original ingredients are not available, technique and ingenuity will overcome the deficiency. This dish is delicious and easy to make, and speaking of adaptability, it can also be made with fresh spinach leaves.

serves 4
preparation time: 20 minutes
cooking time: 20 minutes

2½ lb (1.25 kg) bok choy
  (Chinese white cabbage)
3¾ cups (900 ml) peanut oil
1 teaspoon salt

2 teaspoons sugar
½ cup (50 g) pine nuts,
  lightly roasted

1 Separate the stalks from the stem of the bok choy and then cut the green leaves from the white stalks. (Save the stalks; you can stir-fry them with garlic – see *Stir-fried broccoli* on page 98 – or use them for soup.)

2 Wash the leaves in several changes of cold water, then drain them thoroughly, and dry in a salad spinner. Roll the leaves up tightly, a few at a time, and finely shred them into strips ¼ in (5 mm) wide.

3 Spread them out on a baking sheet and put them in an oven preheated to250°F/ 120°C for 15 minutes to dry slightly. They should not be completely dry or they will burn when fried. Remove from the oven and let them cool. This can be done the day before.

5 Toss the crispy greens with the salt and sugar. Garnish with the pine nuts and serve.

4 Heat a wok over a high heat, then add the oil. When the oil is hot and slightly smoking, deep-fry the greens in 3 or 4 batches. After about 30–40 seconds when they turn crisp and green, remove them immediately from the wok and drain well on paper towels. Let them cool.

Sesame shrimp toast

Sesame shrimp toast is often served as an appetizer in Chinese restaurants. Its origins are rather obscure but I suspect it is a variation on the shrimp paste used widely in southern China as a stuffing or for deep-frying into crispy balls.

makes about 30 pieces
preparation time: 25 minutes
cooking time: 25 minutes

10 thin slices of white bread

3 tablespoons white sesame seeds

2 cups (450 ml) peanut oil

For the shrimp paste:

1 lb (450 g) raw shrimp, shelled and veined (see page 13)

4 oz (100 g) fresh or canned water chestnuts, peeled if fresh, finely chopped

¼ lb (100 g) ground pork

1 teaspoon salt

½ teaspoon freshly ground black pepper

1 egg white

3 tablespoons finely chopped scallions (white part only)

1½ tablespoons finely chopped fresh ginger

1 tablespoon light soy sauce

2 teaspoons sesame oil

2 teaspoons sugar

1 Using a cleaver or sharp knife, chop the shrimp coarsely and then using a food processor, grind them finely into a paste. Put them into a bowl and mix in the rest of the ingredients for the shrimp paste. The paste can be made several hours in advance and kept, covered, in the refrigerator.

2 Remove the crusts from the bread and cut it into rectangles about 3 x 1 in (7.5 x 2.5 cm) – you should have about 3 pieces per slice. If the bread is fresh, place it in a warm oven to dry out a little. Dry bread will absorb less oil.

3 Spread the shrimp paste thickly on each piece of bread. The paste should form a mound about ⅛ in (3 mm) deep, although you can spread it more thinly if you prefer. Sprinkle the toasts with the sesame seeds.

4 Heat the oil over a moderate heat in a wok or deep-fat fryer. Deep-fry several shrimp toasts at a time, paste-side down, for 2–3 minutes. Then turn them over and deep-fry for another 2 minutes until they are golden brown.

5 Remove with a slotted spoon, drain on paper towels, and serve.

Crispy fried wontons

Another favorite with Chinese food lovers. Ordinary wontons become savory treats when dipped in a sweet and sour sauce. They make a great snack or appetizer for any meal. The sauce can be made a day in advance, refrigerated, and then brought to room temperature before serving. The recipe can be doubled easily for those who want more sauce. Wonton skins can be bought fresh or frozen from Asian markets.

8 oz (225 g) wonton skins, thawed if necessary

2½ cups (600 ml) peanut or vegetable oil

For the filling:

¾ cup (350 g) raw shrimp, shelled, veined (see page 13) and coarsely ground or chopped

¼ lb (100 g) ground pork

2 teaspoons salt

½ teaspoon freshly ground black pepper

4 tablespoons finely chopped scallions

2 teaspoons finely chopped fresh ginger

2 teaspoons Shaoxing rice wine or dry sherry

1 teaspoon sugar

2 teaspoons sesame oil

1 egg white, lightly beaten

For the sweet and sour dipping sauce:

⅔ cup (150 ml) water

2 tablespoons sugar

3 tablespoons Chinese white rice vinegar or cider vinegar

3 tablespoons tomato paste or tomato ketchup

1 teaspoon salt

¼ teaspoon freshly ground white pepper

1 teaspoon cornstarch, blended with 2 teaspoons water

serves 6

preparation time: 35 minutes, plus at least 20 minutes' chilling

cooking time: 20 minutes

1 For the filling, put the shrimp and pork in a bowl, add the salt and pepper, and mix well, either by kneading with your hand or stirring with a wooden spoon. Add all the remaining filling ingredients and stir well. Cover with plastic wrap and chill for at least 20 minutes.

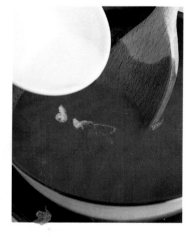

2 In a small saucepan, combine all the ingredients for the sweet and sour sauce except the cornstarch mixture. Bring to a boil, stir in the cornstarch mixture, and cook for 1 minute. Remove from the heat and allow to cool.

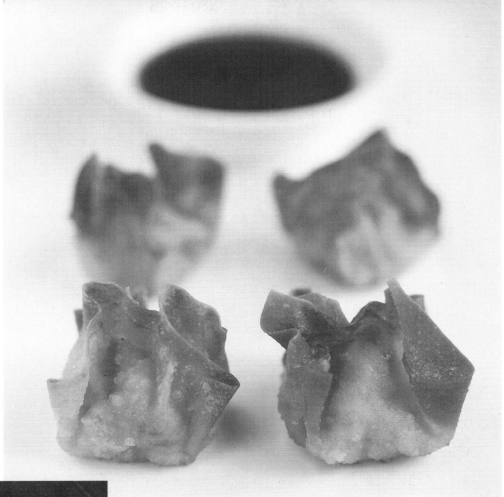

5 Drain the wontons well on paper towels, then serve immediately with the sweet and sour sauce.

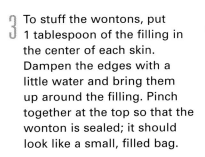

3 To stuff the wontons, put 1 tablespoon of the filling in the center of each skin. Dampen the edges with a little water and bring them up around the filling. Pinch together at the top so that the wonton is sealed; it should look like a small, filled bag.

4 Heat a wok over a high heat. Add the oil, and when it is very hot and slightly smoking, deep-fry the wontons, a handful at a time, for 2–3 minutes or until golden and crisp. If they brown too quickly, reduce the heat slightly.

Dim sum-style pork dumplings

Chinese restaurant diners usually enjoy discovering these tea-house treats, which have always been a favorite of the southern Chinese. They are simply stuffed wontons (egg dough dumplings) that have been steamed instead of poached or deep-fried. Steaming gives them a pronounced, yet subtle, taste and texture. Wonton skins can be obtained fresh or frozen from Asian markets.

1 packet of wonton skins
(about 40), thawed if
necessary

A little vegetable oil

makes about 40
preparation time: 30 minutes
cooking time: 20 minutes
  per batch

For the filling:

4 oz (100 g) fresh or canned
water chestnuts, peeled if
fresh, finely chopped

¼ lb (100 g) raw shrimp,
shelled, veined (see page
13) and coarsely chopped

¾ lb (350 g) ground pork

2 tablespoons finely chopped
prosciutto or lean smoked
bacon

1 tablespoon light soy sauce

1 teaspoon dark soy sauce

1 tablespoon Shaoxing rice
wine or dry sherry

3 tablespoons finely chopped
scallions

2 teaspoons finely chopped
fresh ginger

2 teaspoons sesame oil

1 egg white, lightly beaten

1 teaspoon salt

½ teaspoon freshly ground
black pepper

2 teaspoons sugar

1 To make the filling, put all the ingredients in a bowl and mix together thoroughly.

2 Place a portion of the filling on each wonton skin. Bring up the sides and press them around the filling mixture. Tap the dumpling on the bottom to make a flat base. The top should be wide open, exposing the filling.

3 Set up a steamer or put a rack inside a wok or large, deep pot. Pour in about 2 in (5 cm) of water and bring to a boil. Oil the rack, or the inside of the steamer to keep the dumplings from sticking. Place the dumplings on the rack (you may have to cook them in several batches).

4 Cover the pot tightly, turn the heat to low, and steam gently for about 20 minutes. To save time, use a larger steamer for cooking bigger batches. Serve the dumplings hot; they can be reheated if necessary by steaming gently for a few minutes.

Peking-style caramel walnuts

This Peking-style dish is increasingly popular throughout the West as more non-Cantonese recipes make their way onto Chinese restaurant menus. The shelled walnuts must be blanched first to get rid of any bitterness. Then they are rolled in sugar, left to dry for several hours, and deep-fried to caramelize the sugar coating. Finally, they are rolled in sesame seeds. The result is a classic contrast of tastes and textures. They can be served hot or cold and are perfect with drinks.

2 cups (225 g) shelled walnuts
½ cup (100 g) sugar
2 cups (450 ml) peanut oil
3 tablespoons sesame seeds

serves 4
preparation time: 10 minutes,
  plus at least 2 hours' drying
cooking time: 15 minutes

1 Bring a large pan of water to a boil, add the shelled walnuts, and simmer for about 5 minutes. Drain through a colander or sieve.

2 Pat the walnuts dry with paper towels and spread them on a baking pan. Sprinkle the sugar over the warm nuts and roll them in it to coat them completely. Place the pan in a cool, drafty place, and let them dry for at least 2 hours, preferably overnight. (They can be prepared ahead to this point.)

3 Heat the oil to a moderate heat in a wok or deep-fat fryer. Fry a batch of the walnuts for about 2 minutes or until the sugar melts and the walnuts turn golden (adjust the heat if necessary to prevent burning). Remove the nuts from the oil.

4 Sprinkle the nuts with the sesame seeds and place them on a wire rack to cool. (Do not drain them on paper towels because the sugar will stick when it dries.) Deep-fry and drain the rest of the walnuts in the same way. Serve warm or cold. When they have cooled, the caramel walnuts can be kept in a sealed glass jar for about 2 weeks.

Spring rolls

Spring rolls are one of the best-known Chinese snacks. They are not difficult to make and are a perfect first course for any meal. They should be crisp, light, and delicate. Spring roll skins can be obtained fresh or frozen from Asian markets.

1 packet of spring roll skins, thawed if necessary

1 egg, beaten

4½ cups (1.2 liters) peanut oil for deep-frying

1 quantity of *Sweet and sour dipping sauce* (see page 40)

For the filling:

¼ lb (100 g) raw shrimp, shelled, veined (see page 13), and ground or very finely chopped

¼ lb (100 g) ground pork

1½ tablespoons peanut oil

2 tablespoons coarsely chopped garlic

1 tablespoon finely chopped fresh ginger

1½ tablespoons light soy sauce

1 tablespoon Shaoxing rice wine or dry sherry

3 tablespoons finely chopped scallions

1 teaspoon salt

½ teaspoon freshly ground black pepper

8 oz (225 g) Chinese leaves (Peking cabbage), finely shredded

1 oz (25 g) dried Chinese black mushrooms, soaked, stems removed (see page 11), and finely shredded

For the marinade:

1 teaspoon light soy sauce

1 teaspoon Shaoxing rice wine or dry sherry

1 teaspoon sesame oil

½ teaspoon salt

½ teaspoon freshly ground black pepper

makes about 15–18
preparation time: 40 minutes
cooking time: 20 minutes

1 For the filling, combine the shrimp and pork with all the marinade ingredients in a small bowl.

2 Heat a wok over a high heat. Add the 1½ tablespoons of peanut oil, and when it is very hot and slightly smoking, add the garlic and ginger and stir-fry for 20 seconds.

3 Add all the rest of the filling ingredients, including the shrimp and meat mixture, and stir-fry for 5 minutes. Place the mixture in a colander to drain and allow it to cool thoroughly.

4 Place 3–4 tablespoons of the filling near the end of each spring roll skin, then fold in the sides and roll up tightly.

5 Left: Seal the open end by brushing a small amount of the beaten egg along the edge, then pressing together gently. You should have a roll about 4 in (10 cm) long, a little like an oversized cigar.

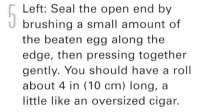

6 Rinse out the wok and reheat it over high heat, then add the oil for deep-frying. When the oil is hot and slightly smoking, gently drop in as many spring rolls as will fit easily in one layer.

7 Fry the spring rolls until golden brown and cooked through, about 4 minutes. Adjust the heat as necessary. Remove with a slotted spoon; drain first on a wire rack and then on paper towels. Cook the remaining spring rolls in the same way. Serve them immediately with the sweet and sour sauce for dipping.

FISH and SHELLFISH

Steamed Cantonese-style fish

Steaming is a favorite Chinese cooking method for fish. A simple but gentle technique, it doesn't mask the fresh taste of the fish, which remains moist and tender, and you can savor the combination of the other ingredients. An added bonus is that it is very healthy. Always buy the freshest possible fish and ask at your fish market to have it prepared for cooking.

serves 4
preparation time: 10 minutes
cooking time: 5–15 minutes

1 lb (450 g) firm white fish fillets, such as cod or sole, skinned, or a whole fish such as sole or turbot

1 teaspoon coarse sea salt or plain salt

1½ tablespoons finely shredded fresh ginger

3 tablespoons finely shredded scallions

2 tablespoons light soy sauce

2 teaspoons dark soy sauce

1 tablespoon peanut oil

2 teaspoons sesame oil

Cilantro sprigs, to garnish

1 Pat the fish dry with paper towels and evenly rub with the salt, rubbing it inside the cavity as well if you are using a whole fish. Put the fish on a heatproof plate and scatter the ginger evenly over the top.

2 Set up a steamer or put a rack into a wok or deep pan. Fill it with 2 in (5 cm) of water and bring to a boil over a high heat. Put the plate of fish on the rack, cover tightly and steam the fish until it is just cooked. Flat fish fillets will take about 5 minutes; whole fish, or fillets such as sea bass, will take 12–14 minutes. The fish should turn opaque and flake slightly but still remain moist.

3 Remove the plate of cooked fish and pour off any liquid that may have accumulated. Scatter the scallions on the fish, then drizzle with the light and dark soy sauces.

4 Heat the two oils together in a small saucepan until smoking, then immediately pour them over the fish. Garnish with cilantro and serve at once.

Sichuan braised fish

This quick and easy dish is bursting with the spicy flavors of Sichuan. A firm, white fish such as cod, sea bass, halibut, or haddock is most suitable for braising.

serves 4
preparation time: 15 minutes
cooking time: 10 minutes

1 lb (450 g) fresh firm white fish fillets, such as cod, sea bass, or halibut, skinned

1 teaspoon salt

Cornstarch for dusting

⅔ cup (150 ml) peanut oil

3 scallions, cut into 2 in (5 cm) slices on the diagonal

1 tablespoon finely chopped garlic

2 teaspoons finely chopped fresh ginger

For the sauce:

⅔ cup (150 ml) *Classic Chinese chicken stock* (see page 26) or good quality ready-made stock

1 teaspoon whole yellow bean sauce

1 tablespoon chili bean sauce

2 tablespoons Shaoxing rice wine or dry sherry

2 teaspoons dark soy sauce

2 teaspoons sugar

2 teaspoons sesame oil

½ teaspoon salt

¼ teaspoon freshly ground white pepper

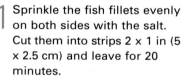

1 Sprinkle the fish fillets evenly on both sides with the salt. Cut them into strips 2 x 1 in (5 x 2.5 cm) and leave for 20 minutes.

2 Dust the strips of fish liberally with cornstarch.

3 Heat a wok over high heat. Add the oil, and when it is hot and slightly smoking, turn the heat down. Fry the pieces of fish on both sides until they are lightly browned. Remove from the wok and drain on paper towels.

4 Pour off most of the oil, leaving about a tablespoon in the wok. Reheat the wok, then add the scallions, garlic, and ginger and stir-fry for 30 seconds.

5 Add all the sauce ingredients and bring to a boil. Turn the heat down to a simmer and return the fish to the pan. Simmer for about 2–3 minutes, then serve.

Sweet and sour shrimp

Perhaps one of the most popular and best known Chinese dishes in the West. It is simple to make, and the sweet, pungent flavors of the sauce combine well with the firm, succulent shrimp.

serves 4
preparation time: 25 minutes
cooking time: 5 minutes

1½ tablespoons peanut oil

1½ tablespoons coarsely chopped garlic

2 teaspoons finely chopped fresh ginger

4 scallions, cut into 1½ in (4 cm) pieces diagonally

1 lb (450 g) raw shrimp, shelled and veined (see page 13)

½ large (100 g) red or green pepper, cut into 1 in (2.5 cm) squares

8 oz (225 g) fresh or canned water chestnuts, peeled if fresh, sliced

For the sauce:

⅔ cup (150 ml) *Classic Chinese chicken stock* (see page 26) or good quality ready-made stock

2 tablespoons Shaoxing rice wine or dry sherry

3 tablespoons light soy sauce

2 teaspoons dark soy sauce

1½ tablespoons tomato paste

3 tablespoons Chinese white rice vinegar or cider vinegar

1 tablespoon sugar

1 tablespoon cornstarch, blended with 2 tablespoons water

1 Heat a wok over high heat, then add the oil. When it is very hot and slightly smoking, add the garlic, ginger, and scallions and stir-fry for 20 seconds.

2 Add the shrimp and stir-fry them for 1 minute.

3 Next add the pepper and water chestnuts and stir-fry for 30 seconds.

4 Now add all the sauce ingredients except the cornstarch
mixture. Bring to a boil, add
the cornstarch mixture, then
turn the heat down and simmer for 3 minutes. Serve
immediately.

Spicy Sichuan-style shrimp

Sichuan cooking is popular throughout China, and in recent years, adventurous Chinese restaurant diners have discovered how delicious it can be. This is one of the best known dishes from that area.

serves 4
preparation time: 25 minutes
cooking time: 5 minutes

1½ tablespoons peanut oil

2 teaspoons finely chopped fresh ginger

1 tablespoon coarsely chopped garlic

2 tablespoons finely chopped scallions

1 lb (450 g) raw shrimp, shelled and veined (see page 13)

For the sauce:

1 tablespoon tomato paste

2 teaspoons chili bean sauce

2 teaspoons Chinese black vinegar or cider vinegar

½ teaspoon salt

½ teaspoon freshly ground black pepper

2 teaspoons sugar

2 teaspoons sesame oil

Cilantro sprigs, to garnish (optional)

1 Heat a wok over a high heat. Add the oil, and when it is very hot and slightly smoking, add the ginger, garlic, and scallions.

2 Stir-fry for 20 seconds, then add the shrimp. Stir-fry the shrimp for about 1 minute.

3 Add all the sauce ingredients and continue to stir-fry for another 3 minutes over a high heat. Serve at once.

Stir-fried squid with vegetables

Squid cooked the Chinese way is both tender and tasty. The secret is to blanch it in boiling water, then cook it for the minimum amount of time – just enough to firm it up slightly. If it is cooked for too long it will become tough, so that eating it is like chewing on rubber bands. This recipe can also be prepared with shrimp if you find squid difficult to obtain.

serves 4
preparation time: 25 minutes
cooking time: 10 minutes

1 lb (450 g) cleaned and prepared squid

1½ tablespoons peanut oil

2 tablespoons coarsely chopped garlic

1 tablespoon finely chopped fresh ginger

½ lb (100 g) red or green pepper, cut into thin strips

1 heaping cup (100 g) snow-peas, trimmed

3 tablespoons *Classic Chinese chicken stock* (see page 26) or good quality ready-made stock

1 tablespoon Shaoxing rice wine or dry sherry

3 tablespoons oyster sauce

1 tablespoon light soy sauce

2 teaspoons dark soy sauce

2 teaspoons salt

2 teaspoons of cornstarch, blended with 2 teaspoons water

2 teaspoons sesame oil

1 If the tentacles are still attached to the head of the squid, cut them off and reserve. Discard the head. Cut the squid bodies into 1½-in (4-cm) strips.

2 Blanch the strips and tentacles by simmering them in a large pan of boiling water for 15 seconds. The squid will firm up slightly and turn an opaque white color. Remove and drain in a colander.

3 Heat a wok over a high heat, and add the oil. When it is very hot and slightly smoking, add the garlic and ginger and stir-fry for 15 seconds. Then add the pepper strips and snowpeas and stir-fry for 1 minute.

4 Add all the rest of the ingredients except the squid and sesame oil and bring the mixture to a boil.

5 Stir it, then add the squid and mix well. Cook for 30 seconds more, stir in the sesame oil, and serve immediately.

Cantonese crab
with black bean sauce

This recipe reflects the popularity of black beans, which go well with almost any food. It is a great favorite in many Chinese restaurants. However, it can only be made with fresh crab in the shell, since the shell protects the delicate crabmeat during the stir-frying process. If you can't get crab in the shell, use shrimp instead. I have added some ground pork – a Chinese trick which helps to stretch the expensive crabmeat. The Chinese tradition-ally eat the crab with their fingers. I suggest you have a large bowl of water decorated with lemon slices on the table so that your guests can rinse their fingers.

serves 4–6
preparation time: 20 minutes
cooking time: 20 minutes

1 live or freshly cooked crab
 in the shell, weighing about
 3 lb (1.5 kg)

2 tablespoons peanut oil

3 tablespoons coarsely
 chopped salted black beans

2 tablespoons coarsely
 chopped garlic

1 tablespoon finely chopped
 fresh ginger

3 tablespoons finely chopped
 scallions

½ lb (225 g) ground pork

2 tablespoons light soy sauce

1 tablespoon dark soy sauce

2 tablespoons Shaoxing rice
 wine or dry sherry

1 cup (250 ml) *Classic
 Chinese chicken stock* (see
 page 26) or good quality
 bought stock

2 eggs, beaten

2 teaspoons sesame oil

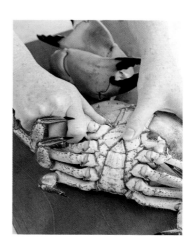

1 To cook a live crab, bring a large pot of water to a boil, add 2 teaspoons of salt and then put in the crab. Cover the pot and cook the crab for about 5–7 minutes, until it turns bright red. Remove with a slotted spoon and drain in a colander. Let the crab cool.

2 Place the cooked crab on its back on a board. Using your fingers, twist the claws from the body. They should come off quite easily.

3 Now twist off the bony tail flap on the underside of the crab and discard it. With your fingers, pry the body from the main shell. Remove and discard the small, bag like stomach sac and its appendages, which are located just behind the crab's mouth.

4 Pull the soft, feathery gills, which look a little like fingers, away from the body and discard them. Remove the legs and put to one side.

5 Using a cleaver or heavy knife, split the crab shell in half and, using a spoon, fork, or skewer, scrape out all the brown crabmeat.

6 Using a cleaver or heavy knife, cut the crab, shell included, into large pieces. Crack the claws and legs slightly.

7 Heat a wok over a high heat. Add the oil, and when it is very hot and slightly smoking, add the black beans, garlic, ginger, and scallions and stir-fry for 20 seconds.

8 Then add the pork and stir-fry for 1 minute. Add the crab pieces and all the remaining ingredients except the eggs and the sesame oil. Stir-fry over a high heat for about 10 minutes.

9 Combine the eggs with the sesame oil and then gradually pour this into the crab mixture, stirring slowly. There should be light strands of egg trailing over the crab mixture. Turn it on to a large, warm platter, or arrange in crab claws and serve.

Steamed fresh oysters

Steaming oysters brings out their subtle, briny taste and wonderful texture. Watch them carefully to prevent over-cooking. This dish is very simple to prepare and makes a dramatic opening for a special dinner party.

serves 4
preparation time: 20 minutes
cooking time: 10 minutes

16 large fresh oysters on the shell

Cilantro sprigs, to garnish

For the sauce:

2 teaspoons finely chopped garlic

1 tablespoon finely chopped fresh ginger

1 teaspoon chili bean sauce

1 tablespoon Shaoxing rice wine or dry sherry

1 tablespoon light soy sauce

2 teaspoons dark soy sauce

2 fresh red chilies, seeded and chopped

3 tablespoons finely shredded scallions

3 tablespoons peanut oil

1 Scrub the oysters clean. You will have to steam them in 2 batches, so divide them between 2 heatproof plates. Next set up a steamer or put a rack into a wok or deep pan and fill it with 2 in (5 cm) of water. Bring the water to a boil over a high heat. Put one plate of oysters into the steamer or on the rack, turn the heat to low, and cover the wok or pan tightly. Steam the oysters gently for 5 minutes or until they are open.

2 Meanwhile, combine all the sauce ingredients except the peanut oil in an oven-proof bowl.

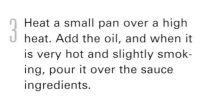

3 Heat a small pan over a high heat. Add the oil, and when it is very hot and slightly smoking, pour it over the sauce ingredients.

4 Remove the oysters from the steamer and cook the second batch. Give the sauce several good stirs. Remove the top shell of each oyster and pour a little sauce over the oysters. Garnish with cilantro sprigs and serve.

MEAT and POULTRY

Stir-fried pork with scallions

This recipe illustrates the relative ease of using a wok. A basic stir-fried meat dish can be made in minutes. The key to success here is not to overcook the pork.

serves 3–4
preparation time: 5 minutes, plus 10–15 minutes' marinating
cooking time: 5–10 minutes

1 lb (450 g) lean boneless pork

1 tablespoon peanut oil

8 scallions, cut on the diagonal into 2 in (5 cm) lengths

1 teaspoon salt

½ teaspoon freshly ground black pepper

1 teaspoon sugar

For the marinade:

1 tablespoon Shaoxing rice wine or dry sherry

1 tablespoon light soy sauce

2 teaspoons sesame oil

1 teaspoon cornstarch

1 Cut the pork into thin slices 2 in (5 cm) long.

2 Put the sliced pork into a bowl and mix in all the marinade ingredients. Leave for 10–15 minutes so that the pork absorbs the flavors of the marinade.

3 Heat a wok to a very high heat, then add the peanut oil. When it is very hot and slightly smoking, add the pork slices and stir-fry for about 2 minutes, until brown. Remove the meat with a slotted spoon and let it drain in a colander.

4 Reheat the wok and add the scallions, salt, pepper and sugar. Stir-fry for 2 minutes or until the scallions are wilted. Return the pork to the wok and stir-fry for another 2 minutes or until heated through. Serve immediately.

Sweet and sour pork, Chiu Chow style

This delicious and unusual version of sweet and sour pork is based on a dish from a region of southern China. It is unlike most of the sweet and sour pork dishes offered in restaurants, which have become clichés bereft of their true character. Here, the ground pork is combined with crisp, sweet water chestnuts, seasoned, and covered in caul fat. This is then dusted with cornstarch and deep-fried. The result is a tender morsel of pork with a light, balanced, sweet and sour flavor.

> serves 4
> preparation time: 35 minutes
> cooking time: 15 minutes

1 lb (450 g) ground pork

1 egg white

4 tablespoons water

6 oz (175 g) fresh or canned water chestnuts, peeled if fresh, coarsely chopped

2 tablespoons light soy sauce

1 tablespoon dark soy sauce

2 tablespoons Shaoxing rice wine or dry sherry

1½ tablespoons sugar

2 teaspoons salt

½ teaspoon freshly ground black pepper

Caul fat for wrapping

¾ cup (100 g) carrots, thinly sliced on the diagonal

½ large (100 g) green pepper, cut into 1-in (2.5-cm) squares

½ large (100 g) red pepper, cut into 1-in (2.5-cm) squares

Cornstarch for dusting

2½ cups (600 ml) peanut oil

4 scallions, cut into 1-in (2.5-cm) pieces

3 oz (75 g) canned lychees, drained, or fresh orange segments

For the sauce:

⅔ cup (150 ml) *Classic Chinese chicken stock* (see page 26) or good quality bought stock

1 tablespoon light soy sauce

2 teaspoons dark soy sauce

2 teaspoons sesame oil

½ teaspoon salt

½ teaspoon freshly ground white pepper

1½ tablespoons Chinese white rice vinegar or cider vinegar

1 tablespoon sugar

2 tablespoons tomato paste or tomato ketchup

2 teaspoons cornstarch, blended with 1 tablespoon water

Cilantro leaves, to garnish (optional)

  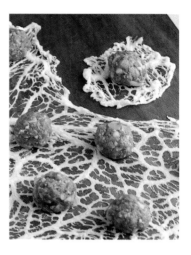

1 Mix the pork, egg white, and water, using your hand (this helps incorporate air). The mixture should be light and fluffy. Do not use a blender since it would make the mixture too dense. Add the water chestnuts, light and dark soy sauce, rice wine or sherry, sugar, salt, and pepper and mix thoroughly.

2 With your hands, shape the mixture into small rounds, about the size of golf balls.

3 Spread out the sheet of caul fat on a work surface and place the pork balls on it at 3-in (7.5-cm) intervals. Then cut the caul fat into 3-in (7.5-cm) squares and wrap it around each pork ball.

4 Bring a pan of water to a boil and blanch the carrots and peppers for about 4 minutes, until barely tender. Drain and set aside.

5 Dust the pork balls with cornstarch, shaking off any excess. Heat the oil in a deep-fat fryer or large wok until slightly smoking. Reduce the heat to moderate and deep-fry the pork balls for 3–4 minutes, until crisp and cooked through. Remove with a slotted spoon and drain on paper towels.

6 In a large saucepan, combine all the sauce ingredients except the cornstarch mixture and bring to a boil. Add the peppers, carrots and scallions and stir well. Stir in the cornstarch mixture and cook for 2 minutes, then turn the heat down so that the mixture is simmering. Add the lychees or orange segments and the pork balls to the sauce. Mix well, then serve immediately.

Crackling Chinese roast pork

One of the most fascinating sights in Chinatowns all over the world is shops with whole roast adult pigs as well as suckling pigs hanging in the window. The meat is delicious with rice or in stir-fried dishes. The secret of crispy skin is to blanch it and then let it dry using a technique similar to the one used for *Peking duck* (see page 90). Then the skin is slowly roasted so that most of fat runs off, leaving soft, tender pork flesh marbled with velvety fat. No wonder most diners are addicted to this delicious dish after the first bite. Much of the work can be done ahead of time, and it is surprisingly easy.

serves 4–6
preparation time: 15 minutes,
    plus drying overnight
cooking time: 2½ hours

3 lb (1.5 kg) boneless pork belly, with rind

For the dry rub:

2 tablespoons coarse sea salt

1 tablespoon ground roasted Sichuan peppercorns (see page 15)

2 teaspoons five-spice powder

1 teaspoon freshly ground black pepper

2 teaspoons sugar

Perfect steamed rice to serve (optional, see page 110)

1 Pierce the rind side of the pork with a sharp fork or knife until the skin is covered with fine holes. Insert a meat hook into the pork.

2 Bring a large pan of water to a boil. Hang the pork up from the meat hook, and using a large ladle, pour the hot water over the rind side several times. Set the pork aside.

5 Turn up the heat to 450°F/ 230°C and roast for a final fifteen minutes. Remove the pork and let it cool. Carve it into bite-sized pieces, arrange on a platter and serve. Alternatively, serve on beds of rice as shown.

3 Heat a wok, then add all the ingredients for the dry rub and stir-fry for 3 minutes until they are well mixed. Let cool slightly.When the dry rub is cool enough to handle, rub it all over the flesh side of the pork.

4 Hang the meat up to dry for eight hours or overnight in a cool place or in front of a cold fan. Preheat the oven to 400°F/200°C. Place the pork, rind side up, on a rack over a roasting tin of water. Roast for 15 minutes, then reduce the heat to 350°F/180°C and continue to roast for 2 hours.

Stir-fried beef
with oyster sauce

This used to be one of the most popular dishes in my family's restaurant, especially with Westerners. It is very savory and quite addictive. Buy the best brand of oyster sauce you can find. Good oyster sauce does not taste at all fishy. Rather, it has a meaty flavor and goes very well with beef or pork. This simple dish is delicious served with plain steamed rice.

1 lb (450 g) lean beef steak

1 tablespoon light soy sauce

2 teaspoons sesame oil

1 tablespoon Shaoxing rice wine or dry sherry

2 teaspoons cornstarch

3 tablespoons peanut oil

3 tablespoons oyster sauce

1½ tablespoons finely chopped scallions, to garnish

serves 4
preparation time: 10 minutes, plus 20 minutes' marinating
cooking time: 10 minutes

1 Cut the beef into slices 2 in (5 cm) long and ¼ in (5 mm) thick, cutting against the grain of the meat. Put them into a bowl.

2 Mix in the soy sauce, sesame oil, rice wine or sherry, and cornstarch. Let the meat marinate for 20 minutes.

3 Heat a wok until it is very hot, then add the peanut oil. When it is very hot and slightly smoking, add the beef slices and stir-fry for 5 minutes or until lightly browned.

4 Remove the meat from the wok and drain well in a colander set over a bowl. Discard the drained oil.

5 Wipe the wok clean and reheat it over a high heat. Add the oyster sauce and bring it to a simmer.

6 Return the drained beef slices to the wok and toss them thoroughly with the oyster sauce. Turn the mixture on to a serving platter, garnish with the scallions, and serve immediately.

Stir-fried chicken with black bean sauce

This is a favorite of many first-time diners in Chinese restaurants, and no wonder. The fragrance of fermented black bean sauce mixed with garlic and ginger is mouthwatering.
It can be cooked ahead of time and reheated, and it is also delicious served cold.

1 lb (450 g) boneless skinless chicken breasts, cut into 2 in (5 cm) chunks

1 tablespoon light soy sauce

1½ tablespoons Shaoxing rice wine or dry sherry

½ teaspoon salt

1 teaspoon sugar

1 teaspoon sesame oil

2 teaspoons cornstarch

2 tablespoons peanut oil

1 tablespoon finely chopped fresh ginger

1½ tablespoons coarsely chopped garlic

2 tablespoons finely chopped shallots

3½ tablespoons finely chopped scallions

2½ tablespoons coarsely chopped salted black beans

⅔ cup (150 ml) *Classic Chinese chicken stock* (see page 26) or good quality ready-made stock

serves 4
preparation time: 15 minutes
cooking time: 10 minutes

1 Put the chicken in a bowl and mix with the soy sauce, rice wine or sherry, salt, sugar, sesame oil, and cornstarch.

2 Heat a wok over a high heat, then add the oil. When it is very hot and slightly smoking, add the chicken and stir-fry for 2 minutes.

3 Then add the ginger, garlic, shallots, 1½ tablespoons of the scallions, and the black beans and stir-fry for 2 minutes.

4 Finally, add the stock. Bring the mixture to a boil, then reduce the heat, cover, and simmer for 3 minutes or until the chicken is cooked. Garnish with the remaining scallions and serve.

Spicy chicken with peanuts

This classic western Chinese dish is better known as *gongbao* or *kung pao* chicken. There are many versions of this recipe; this one is close to the original and is also easy to make.

serves 4
preparation time: 15 minutes
cooking time: 5–10 minutes

3 tablespoons peanut oil

3 dried red chilies, split lengthwise in half

1 lb (450 g) boneless skinless chicken breasts, cut into 1-in (2.5-cm) chunks

¾ cup (75 g) roasted peanuts

For the sauce:

2 tablespoons *Classic Chinese chicken stock* (see page 26) or good quality ready-made stock

2 tablespoons Shaoxing rice wine or dry sherry

1 tablespoon dark soy sauce

2 teaspoons sugar

1 tablespoon coarsely chopped garlic

2 teaspoons finely chopped scallions

1 teaspoon finely chopped fresh ginger

2 teaspoons Chinese white rice vinegar or cider vinegar

1 teaspoon salt

2 teaspoons sesame oil

1 Heat a wok over a high heat. Add the oil and chilies and stir-fry for a few seconds (you may remove the chilies when they turn black or leave them in).

2 Next add the chicken and peanuts, and stir-fry for 1 minute. Remove the chicken, peanuts and chilies from the wok and drain in a colander.

3 Put all the sauce ingredients except the sesame oil into the wok. Bring to a boil and then turn the heat down.

4 Return the chicken, peanuts, and chilies to the wok and cook for about 3–4 minutes in the sauce, mixing well.

5 Finally, add the sesame oil. Give the mixture a good stir and remove the chilies, if you prefer; serve immediately.

Classic lemon chicken

The southern Chinese have made a speciality of chicken cooked with lemon. The tart sauce goes very well indeed with the receptive flavor of chicken. Unlike many versions, which employ a cloyingly sweet sauce, this recipe balances tartness with sweetness. Sometimes the lemon chicken is battered and deep-fried, but I think it is equally good stir-fried, especially if the chicken is "velveted" in hot oil or water beforehand.

serves 4
preparation time: 15 minutes,
plus 20 minutes' chilling
cooking time: 10 minutes

1 lb (450 g) boneless, skinless chicken breasts, cut into strips 3 in (7.5 cm) long x ½ (1 cm) thick

1 egg white

1 teaspoon salt

1 teaspoon sesame oil

2 teaspoons cornstarch

1¼ cups (300 ml) peanut oil or water

2 tablespoons finely chopped scallions, to garnish

For the sauce:

⅓ cup (65 ml) *Classic Chinese chicken stock* (see page 26) or good quality ready-made stock

3 tablespoons fresh lemon juice

1 tablespoon sugar

1 tablespoon light soy sauce

1½ tablespoons Shaoxing rice wine or dry sherry

1½ tablespoons finely chopped garlic

1–2 teaspoons crushed dried red chili

1 teaspoon cornstarch, blended with 1 teaspoon water

2 teaspoons sesame oil

1 Put the chicken strips in a bowl and combine with the egg white, salt, sesame oil, and cornstarch. Put the mixture in the refrigerator for about 20 minutes.

2 If you are using oil for velveting the chicken, heat a wok until very hot, and then add the oil. When it is very hot, remove from the heat and immediately add the chicken, stirring vigorously to prevent it from sticking. After about 2 minutes, when the chicken turns white, quickly pour it through a stainless steel colander set over a bowl to drain off the oil, which should be discarded. If using water for velveting the chicken, follow the same procedure, but bring the water to a boil in a saucepan before adding the chicken. It will take about 4 minutes to turn white in the water.

3 If you have used a wok, wipe it clean. Heat it, then add all the sauce ingredients except the cornstarch mixture and sesame oil. Bring to a boil over a high heat and then add the cornstarch mixture. Simmer for 1 minute.

4 Return the chicken strips to the wok and stir-fry long enough to coat them all with the sauce. Mix in the sesame oil, then turn onto a platter, garnish with the scallions and serve immediately.

Chinese chicken curry

Curry blends well with chicken, especially when used Chinese style as a light, subtle sauce that does not overpower the delicate taste of the meat. The chicken is 'velveted' before cooking to preserve its juiciness and flavor. You can do this by the traditional oil method or, for a less fattening dish, substitute water instead. This curry is mild, unlike traditional Indian curry.

serves 4
preparation time: 15 minutes,
  plus 20 minutes' chilling
cooking time: 10 minutes

1 lb (450 g) boneless, skinless chicken breasts, cut into 1-in (2.5-cm) chunks

1 egg white

1 teaspoon salt

1 teaspoon sesame oil

3 teaspoons cornstarch

1¼ cups (300 ml) peanut oil or water

1 tablespoon peanut oil

8 oz (225 g) red or green peppers, cut into 1-in (2.5-cm) pieces

1 tablespoon coarsely chopped garlic

⅔ cup (150 ml) *Classic Chinese chicken stock* (see page 26) or good quality ready-made stock

1½ tablespoons Madras curry paste or powder

2 teaspoons sugar

1½ tablespoons Shaoxing rice wine or dry sherry

1½ tablespoons light soy sauce

1 teaspoon cornstarch, blended with 1 tablespoon water

Cilantro leaves, to garnish (optional)

1 Put the chicken pieces into a bowl with the egg white, salt, sesame oil, and 2 teaspoons of the cornstarch; mix well. Put the mixture into the refrigerator for about 20 minutes.

2 If you are using oil for velveting the chicken, heat a wok until very hot and then add the oil. When it is very hot, remove the wok from the heat and immediately add the chicken, stirring vigorously to prevent it sticking. After about 2 minutes, when the chicken turns white, quickly drain it and all of the oil in a stainless steel colander set over a bowl. Discard the oil. If you are using water, do exactly the same, but bring the water to a boil in a saucepan before adding the chicken. It will take about 4 minutes to turn white in the water.

3 If you have used the wok, wipe it clean. Heat it until it is very hot, then add the tablespoon of peanut oil. When it is very hot, add the peppers and garlic, and stir-fry for 2 minutes.

4 Add the stock, curry paste or powder, sugar, rice wine or sherry, soy sauce, and cornstarch mixture. Cook for 2 minutes. Add the drained chicken to the wok and stir-fry for another 2 minutes, coating the chicken thoroughly with the sauce. Serve immediately.

CHINESE CHICKEN CURRY |

Cashew chicken

This exemplifies the Chinese penchant for contrasting textures. Tender, succulent pieces of chicken are combined with sweet, crunchy cashew nuts. The secret to this popular dish is the use of that wonderful technique, velveting, in hot oil or water, which seals in the juices of the chicken, and then stir-frying as a second step to give it that unique taste.

serves 4
preparation time: 10 minutes
cooking time: 5–10 minutes

1 lb (450 g) boneless, skinless chicken breasts, cut into ½-in (1-cm) chunks

1 egg white

1 teaspoon salt

1 teaspoon sesame oil

2 teaspoons cornstarch

1¼ cups (300 ml) peanut oil or water

2 teaspoons peanut oil

½ cup (50 g) cashew nuts

1 tablespoon Shaoxing rice wine or dry sherry

1 tablespoon light soy sauce

1 tablespoon finely shredded scallions, to garnish

1 Put the chicken in a bowl with the egg white, salt, sesame oil, and cornstarch; mix well. Put the mixture in the refrigerator for about 20 minutes.

2 If you are using oil for velveting the chicken, heat a wok until very hot and then add the oil. When it is very hot, remove the wok from the heat and immediately add the chicken, stirring vigorously to prevent it sticking. After about 2 minutes, when the chicken turns white, quickly drain it and all of the oil through a stainless steel colander set over a bowl. Discard the oil. If you are using water (as above), do exactly the same but bring the water to a boil in a saucepan before adding the chicken. It will take about 4 minutes to turn white in the water.

3 If you have used a wok, wipe it clean. Heat it until it is very hot, then add the 2 teaspoons of peanut oil. Add the cashew nuts and stir-fry them for 1 minute.

4 Add the rice wine or dry sherry and soy sauce. Return the chicken to the wok and stir-fry for 2 minutes. Garnish with the scallions and serve immediately.

Peking duck

This is one of the most admired of all Chinese dishes. Certainly it is the one that captures everyone's fantasy of great Chinese food. How can one resist rich, succulent duck meat and crispy, crackling skin?

serves 4–6

preparation time: 20 minutes, plus at least 4 hours' drying

cooking time: 1½ hours

The classic preparation and cooking of Peking duck is an art form. Hot water combined with soy sauce and vinegar is poured over the duck to close the pores, then the bird is hung up to dry. During the drying process, a solution of malt sugar is liberally brushed over the duck, which is then roasted in wood-burning ovens. The result is a shiny, crisp, aromatic bird with beautiful brown skin, moist flesh and no fat.

Preparing Peking duck is a time consuming task but I have devised a simpler method that gives impressive results, closely approximating the real thing. Just allow yourself plenty of time and the dish will be good enough for an emperor. If possible, use a plump, meaty duck, such as Cherry Valley, which is available from most large supermarkets.

Traditionally Peking duck is served with Chinese pancakes, shredded scallions and sweet bean sauce. In Hong Kong and the West hoisin sauce is used instead. This is very similar to sweet bean sauce but contains vinegar. Each guest spoons some sauce on to a pancake, then places a helping of crisp skin and meat on top with some scallion shreds and cucumber sticks. The entire mixture is rolled up in the pancake and then eaten using chopsticks or one's fingers. It makes an unforgettable dish for a special dinner party.

1 If the duck is frozen, thaw it thoroughly. Rinse it well and blot completely dry with paper towels. Insert a meat hook near the neck. Combine the ingredients for the honey syrup in a large wok or pan and bring to a boil. Holding the duck up by the meat hook, use a large ladle or spoon to pour the syrup over the duck several times, as if to bathe it, until the skin is completely coated with the mixture. Once used, the mixture can be discarded.

1 x 6 lb (2.75 kg) duck, fresh or frozen, preferably Cherry Valley

For the honey syrup:

2 tablespoons cider vinegar

4½ cups (1.2 liters) water

3 tablespoons honey

3 tablespoons dark soy sauce

To serve:

Chinese pancakes (see page 106)

4 scallions, finely shredded

1 cucumber, peeled, deseeded and cut into 2 x 1-in (5 x 2.5-cm) pieces

6 tablespoons hoisin sauce or sweet bean sauce

2 Hang the duck to dry in a cool, well ventilated place, or hang it in front of a cold fan for about 4-5 hours, longer if possible. Be sure to put a roasting pan underneath to catch any drips. Once the duck has dried, the skin will feel like parchment.

3 Preheat the oven to 475°F/240°C. Place the duck, breast side up, on a rack in a roasting pan. Put ⅔ cup (150 ml) of water into the pan to keep the fat from splattering. Now put the duck into the oven and roast it for 15 minutes. Turn the heat down to 350°F/180°C and continue to roast for 1 hour and 10 minutes. Replenish the water as necessary.

4 Remove the duck from the oven and let it rest for at least 10 minutes before you carve it. Using a cleaver or a sharp knife, cut the skin and meat into pieces and arrange them on a warm platter. Serve immediately, with the Chinese pancakes, scallions, cucumber, and a bowl of hoisin sauce or sweet bean sauce.

Crispy aromatic duck

This is probably one of the best-selling dishes in Chinese restaurants in the West. Although it is available as a ready-made meal, nothing beats the homemade version. Don't be intimidated by the long preparation process. Most of the steps are quite straightforward and can be done up to a day in advance, and the results are well worth the labor. Steaming the duck renders out most of the fat, leaving the meat moist and succulent. The final deep-frying crisps the skin beautifully.

serves 4–6
preparation time: 15 minutes, plus 2 hours' cooling
cooking time: 2½ hours

1 x 6 lb (2.75 kg) duck, fresh or frozen, preferably Cherry Valley
6 slices of fresh ginger, 3 x ¼ in (7.5 cm x 5 mm)
6 scallions, cut into 3-in (7.5-cm) lengths
Cornstarch, all-purpose flour or potato flour for dusting
4½ cups (1.2 liters) peanut oil

For the spice rub:
2 tablespoons five-spice powder
5 tablespoons (65 g) Sichuan peppercorns
1 oz (25 g) whole black peppercorns
3 tablespoons cumin seeds
7 tablespoons (200 g) rock or sea salt

To serve:
Chinese pancakes (see page 105)
6 scallions, finely shredded
Hoisin sauce

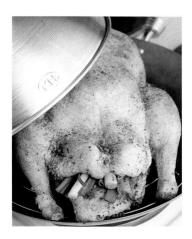

1 | If the duck is frozen, thaw it thoroughly. Rinse well and blot it completely dry with paper towels. Mix all the ingredients for the spice rub together in a small bowl, then rub the duck inside and out with this mixture, applying it evenly. Wrap well in plastic wrap and place in the refrigerator for 24 hours.

2 | After this time, brush any excess spices from the duck. Stuff the ginger and scallions into the cavity and put the duck on an ovenproof plate. Set up a steamer or put a rack into a wok. Fill it with 2 in (5 cm) of water and bring to a boil. Lower the plate with the duck into the steamer and cover tightly.

3 | Steam gently for 2 hours, pouring off excess fat from time to time. Add more water as necessary. Remove the duck from the steamer and pour off all the liquid. Discard the ginger and scallions. Leave the duck in a cool place for 2 hours or until it has dried and cooled. At this point the duck can be refrigerated.

4 | Just before you are ready to serve it, cut the duck into quarters and dust with cornstarch, all-purpose flour or potato flour, shaking off the excess.

5 | Heat the oil in a wok or deep-fat fryer. When it is almost smoking, deep-fry the duck quarters in 2 batches. Fry the breasts for about 8–10 minutes and the thighs and legs for about 12–15 minutes, until each quarter is crisp and heated right through.

6 | Drain the duck on paper towels and let it cool enough to handle. Then remove the meat from the bones and shred it. You can do this easily with a fork. The Chinese eat it with bones and all. Serve with the Chinese pancakes, scallions, and hoisin sauce.

VEGETABLES and SIDE DISHES

Stir-fried spinach

This is a perfect way to cook vegetables such as spinach that contain a great deal of moisture. The technique is to place the spinach in a very hot wok and quickly stir-fry with some seasoning. It is that simple to prepare and may be served hot or cold.

24 cups (675 g) fresh spinach

1 tablespoon peanut oil

2 tablespoons coarsely chopped garlic

1 teaspoon salt

1 teaspoon sugar

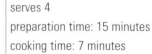

serves 4

preparation time: 15 minutes

cooking time: 7 minutes

1 Wash the spinach thoroughly. Remove all the stems, leaving just the leaves.

2 Heat a wok over a high heat. Add the oil, and when it is very hot and slightly smoking, add the garlic and salt. Stir-fry for 10 seconds.

3 Add the spinach and stir-fry for about 2 minutes, until the leaves are thoroughly coated with the oil, garlic, and salt.

4 When the spinach has wilted to about one-third of its original size, add the sugar and stir-fry for another 4 minutes. Transfer the spinach to a serving dish and pour off any excess liquid. Serve immediately.

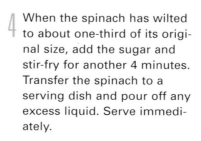

Stir-fried broccoli

Stir-frying is one of the most appealing cooking techniques for this colorful and extraordinarily nutritious vegetable. The secret of making this simple dish is to add a little water and cover the wok tightly, so the broccoli can cook to perfection.

About ½ of 1 lb (450 g) a
    broccoli head

1½ tablespoons peanut oil

4 garlic cloves, lightly
    crushed

1 teaspoon salt

½ teaspoon freshly ground
    black pepper

6 tablespoons water

2 teaspoons sesame oil

serves 4
preparation time: 10 minutes
cooking time: 6 minutes

1 Cut the stems off the broccoli and separate the heads into small florets. Peel and slice the stems.

2 Heat a wok over a high heat. Add the peanut oil, and when it is very hot and slightly smoking, add the garlic, salt, and pepper. Stir-fry for 30 seconds, or until the garlic is lightly browned.

3 Add the broccoli and stir-fry for 2 minutes. Now add the water, cover tightly, and cook over a high heat for 4–5 minutes.

4 Uncover and test the broccoli
by gently piercing it with the
tip of a sharp knife; the knife
should go in quite easily. Stir
in the sesame oil and stir-fry
for 30 seconds, then serve.

Stir-fried mixed vegetables

Stir-fried vegetable dishes should not contain more than four or five types of vegetable, and these vegetables should be varied – some crisp, like green beans, others leafy, such as spinach. The art of stir-frying vegetables is knowing when to add them to the wok. If you throw them all in at once they might become soggy, regardless of their water content. Put the tougher, more textured ones in the wok first to give them a head start. The amount of cooking water you need to add depends on how much natural water is in the vegetables you are using. Make sure you add only the minimum amount (no more than 1–2 tablespoons) if you are using the wok covered, otherwise the vegetables will oversteam and become soggy.

serves 4
preparation time: 15 minutes
cooking time: 7 minutes

1 cup (225 g) Chinese leaves (Peking cabbage)

1 cup (225 g) Chinese greens, such as Chinese flowering cabbage, pak choy, or spinach

½ bunch (225 g) asparagus

4 (225 g) carrots

1½ tablespoons peanut oil

2 tablespoons coarsely chopped shallots

2 tablespoons coarsely chopped garlic

2 teaspoons finely chopped fresh ginger

2 teaspoons salt

1–2 tablespoons water

2 teaspoons sugar

1 tablespoon Shaoxing rice wine or dry sherry

2 teaspoons sesame oil

1 Cut the Chinese leaves into 1½-in (4-cm) strips. Then cut the greens and asparagus into 1½-in (4-cm) pieces. Cut the carrots on the diagonal into slices ¼ in (5 mm) thick.

2 Heat a wok over a high heat. Add the peanut oil, and when it is very hot and slightly smoking, add the shallots, garlic, ginger, and salt, and stir-fry for 1 minute.

3 Then add the carrots and asparagus and stir-fry for 30 seconds. Add the water, cover, and cook over a high heat for 2 minutes.

4 Add the Chinese leaves and greens, along with the sugar and rice wine or sherry. Stir-fry for 3 minutes or until the greens are thoroughly wilted. Then add the sesame oil and serve at once.

Braised Sichuan-style spicy beancurd

This traditional dish from Sichuan province in China is becoming popular in the West. Bland but very healthy beancurd is mixed with spicy, fragrant ingredients to produce a sensational dish that is simply mouthwatering. The essence of this recipe lies in the quality of the seasonings, condiments, and the care taken in cooking them just right.

serves 4
preparation time: 5 minutes
cooking time: 6 minutes

1 lb (450 g) fresh beancurd

1 tablespoon peanut oil

1 tablespoon whole yellow bean sauce

1 tablespoon dark soy sauce

½ teaspoon salt

1 teaspoon red chili powder or cayenne pepper, to taste

¾ cup (175 ml) *Classic Chinese chicken stock* (see page 26) or good quality ready-made stock

2 tablespoons coarsely chopped garlic

2 teaspoons cornstarch, mixed with 1 tablespoon water

1 teaspoon finely ground roasted Sichuan peppercorns (see page 15)

1 Gently cut the beancurd into 1½-in (4-cm) cubes.

2 Heat a wok, add the peanut oil and yellow bean sauce and stir-fry for 30 seconds. Add the soy sauce and salt and stir-fry for 1 minute.

3 Add the chili powder and stir-fry for 30 seconds. Then pour in the stock, add the beancurd and simmer for 3 minutes.

4 Finally, stir in the garlic and the cornstarch mixture and cook for 1 minute. Ladle the mixture into a serving bowl, sprinkle over the ground Sichuan peppercorns and serve at once.

Sichuan-style green beans

This delectable dish originated in western China, as its seasonings indicate. The traditional recipe calls for Chinese asparagus or long beans, but I find green beans equally suitable. They are deep-fried to give them a soft rather than a crunchy texture, but they should remain green and not be overcooked. After deep-frying, the beans are stir-fried in an array of spices. They should be slightly oily, but if they are too oily for your taste you can blot them with paper towels before stir-frying them. For best results, serve the beans as soon as they are cooked. A delicious vegetarian dish.

serves 4
preparation time: 10 minutes
cooking time: 10 minutes

2½ cups (600 ml) peanut oil

1 lb (450 g) green beans, sliced if long, left whole otherwise

2 tablespoons coarsely chopped garlic

1 tablespoon finely chopped fresh ginger

3 tablespoons finely chopped scallions (white part only)

1½ tablespoons chili bean sauce

1 tablespoon whole yellow bean sauce

2 tablespoons Shaoxing rice wine or dry sherry

1 tablespoon dark soy sauce

2 teaspoons sugar

1 tablespoon water

2 teaspoons chili oil

1 Heat a wok over a high heat. Add the oil and when it is very hot and slightly smoking, deep-fry half the beans until slightly wrinkled, which should take about 3–4 minutes. Remove the beans and drain them. Deep-fry the second batch in the same way.

2 Transfer about 1 tablespoon of the oil in which you have cooked the beans to a clean wok or frying-pan. Heat the oil, then add the garlic, ginger, and scallions and stir-fry for 30 seconds.

3 Add all the rest of the ingredients except the green beans and stir-fry for 30 seconds.

4 Add the drained beans and mix until they are thoroughly coated with the spicy mixture. Serve as soon as the beans have heated through.

Chinese pancakes

These pancakes are the classic accompaniment to Peking Duck (see page 90) and Crispy Aromatic Duck (see page 92); they reflect the northern Chinese use of wheat instead of rice. With practice, they are easy to make. The unusual method of rolling "double" pancakes is designed to ensure thinner, moister pancakes with less risk of overcooking them. They can be wrapped tightly in plastic wrap and frozen, so you can make them weeks in advance.

To reheat the pancakes, steam them briefly, or you could cover them tightly with plastic wrap and microwave them – this takes only a minute. Don't be tempted to reheat them in the oven because this will dry them out too much. If you are using pancakes that have been frozen, let them thaw in the refrigerator before reheating.

> serves 6–8
> preparation time: 40 minutes,
>   plus 30 minutes' resting
>   the dough
> cooking time: 20–30 minutes

2¾ cups (275 g) all-purpose
  flour, plus extra for dusting
1 cup (250 ml) very hot water
2 tablespoons sesame oil

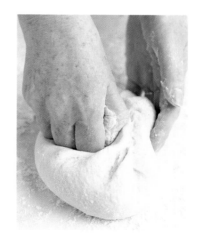

1 Put the flour into a large bowl. Gradually stir in the hot water, mixing all the while with chopsticks or a fork until it is fully incorporated. Add more water if the mixture seems dry.

2 Turn the dough out and knead it with your hands for about 8 minutes or until it is smooth, dusting with flour if necessary, since it may be quite sticky at this point. Put the dough back into the bowl, cover it with a damp kitchen towel and let it rest for about 30 minutes.

3 Remove the dough from the bowl and knead it again for about 5 minutes, dusting with a little flour if it is sticky. Once the dough is smooth, form it into a roll about 18 in (45 cm) long and 1 in (2.5 cm) thick. Cut the roll into 18 equal pieces and shape each one into a ball.

4 Take 2 of the dough balls. Dip one side of one ball into the sesame oil and place the oiled side on top of the other ball.

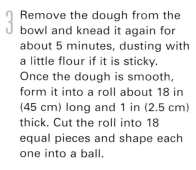

7 Right: Remove from the pan and let it cool slightly. When it is still warm, but cool enough to handle, peel the 2 pancakes apart and set them aside. Repeat this process until all the pancakes have been cooked.

5 With a rolling pin, roll the 2 pancakes simultaneously into a circle about 6 in (15 cm) in diameter. You can flip the double pancake over and roll on the other side as well.

6 Heat a frying-pan or wok over a very low flame. Put the double pancake into the pan and cook it for 1–2 minutes, until it becomes dry and flecked with brown. Flip it over and cook the other side the same way.

Perfect steamed rice

The Chinese way of steaming rice is simple, direct and effective. I prefer to use long-grain white rice, which is dry and fluffy when cooked. Don't use precooked or "instant" rice because it lacks the texture and starchy taste fundamental to Chinese rice.

The secret of preparing rice without it becoming sticky is to cook it first in an uncovered pan at a high heat until most of the water has evaporated. Then the heat should be turned very low, the pan covered, and the rice cooked slowly in the remaining steam. Never uncover the pan once the steaming process has begun; just time it and wait.

Here is a good trick to remember: if you cover the rice with about 1 in (2.5 cm) of water it should always cook properly without sticking. Many recipes on packages of rice call for too much water and result in a gluey mess. Follow my method and you will easily have perfect steamed rice, the Chinese way.

serves 4
preparation time: 20 minutes
cooking time: 20 minutes

Enough long-grain rice to fill
    a glass measuring cup to 1¾
    cups (400 ml)
2½ cups (600 ml) water

1 Put the rice into a large bowl and wash it in several changes of water until the water becomes clear.

2 Drain the rice. Put in a heavy pan with the 2½ cups (600 ml) water and bring to a boil. Boil for about 5 minutes until most of the surface liquid has evaporated. The surface of the rice should have small indentations like a pitted crater.

3 At this point, cover the pan with a very tight fitting lid, turn the heat as low as possible and let the rice cook undisturbed for 15 minutes. There is no need to 'fluff' the rice; just let it rest off the heat for 5 minutes before serving.

Egg-fried rice

Egg fried rice is common in Chinese restaurants and is probably the best known Chinese dish in the West. The secret is to use cold cooked rice and a very hot wok. Remember that authentic fried rice should have a wonderful smoky taste, and should never be greasy or heavy.

serves 4
preparation time: 5 minutes
cooking time: 8 minutes

2 large eggs, lightly beaten

2 teaspoons sesame oil

1 teaspoon salt

2 tablespoons peanut oil

1 recipe of *Perfect steamed rice* (see page 110), cooled completely

¼ teaspoon freshly ground black pepper

2 tablespoons finely chopped scallions

3 Next, drizzle the egg and oil mixture over the rice and continue to stir-fry for 2–3 minutes or until the eggs are set and the mixture is dry.

4 Add the remaining salt and the pepper and stir-fry for 2 minutes longer, then toss in the scallions. Stir several times, turn onto a platter, and serve at once.

1 Put the eggs, sesame oil, and half the salt in a small bowl, mix with a fork, and set aside.

2 Heat a wok over a high heat. Add the peanut oil and when it is very hot and slightly smoking, add the cold cooked rice. Stir-fry for 3 minutes, or until it is thoroughly heated.

Chow mein

Chow mein literally means "stir-fried noodles" and this dish is as popular in the West as it is in southern China. It is a quick and delicious way to prepare egg noodles. Almost any ingredient you like, such as fish, meat, poultry, or vegetables, can be added to it. It makes a popular lunch dish, either served at the end of the meal or eaten by itself.

serves 4
preparation time: 10 minutes,
 plus 10 minutes' marinating
cooking time: 20 minutes

8 oz (225 g) dried or fresh
  egg noodles

4 teaspoons sesame oil

¼ lb (100 g) boneless, skinless chicken breasts, cut into fine shreds 2 in (5 cm) long

2½ tablespoons peanut oil

1 tablespoon finely chopped garlic

About ½ heaping cup (50 g) snowpeas, finely shredded

2 oz (50 g) prosciutto or cooked ham, finely shredded

2 teaspoons light soy sauce

2 teaspoons dark soy sauce

1 tablespoon Shaoxing rice wine or dry sherry

1 teaspoon salt

½ teaspoon freshly ground white pepper

½ teaspoon sugar

3 tablespoons finely chopped scallions

For the marinade:

2 teaspoons light soy sauce

2 teaspoons Shaoxing rice wine or dry sherry

1 teaspoon sesame oil

½ teaspoon salt

½ teaspoon freshly ground white pepper

1 Cook the noodles in a large pot of boiling water for 3–5 minutes, then drain and plunge them into cold water. Drain thoroughly, toss them with 3 teaspoons of the sesame oil, and set aside.

2 Combine the chicken shreds with all the marinade ingredients, mix well and then let marinate for about 10 minutes.

3 Heat a wok over a high heat. Add 1 tablespoon of the peanut oil and when it is very hot and slightly smoking, add the chicken shreds. Stir-fry for about 2 minutes and then transfer to a plate. Wipe the wok clean.

4 Reheat the wok until it is very hot, then add the remaining peanut oil. When the oil is slightly smoking, add the garlic and stir-fry for 10 seconds. Then add the snowpeas and ham and stir-fry for about 1 minute more.

5 Left: Add the noodles, soy sauces, rice wine or sherry, salt, pepper, sugar, and scallions. Stir-fry for 2 minutes.

6 Return the chicken and any juices to the noodle mixture. Stir-fry for about 3–4 minutes or until the chicken is cooked.

7 Add the remaining sesame oil and give the mixture a few final stirs. Turn it onto a warm platter and serve at once.

Northern-style cold noodles

These savory noodles are perfect for any meal or snack. They are quick and easy to make but if you wish to prepare them ahead of time, keep the sauce and noodles separate until the last possible moment.

serves 4
preparation time: 10 minutes
cooking time: 3–5 minutes

12 oz (350 g) dried or fresh egg noodles

2 tablespoons sesame oil

3 tablespoons finely chopped scallions, to garnish

For the sauce:

3 tablespoons sesame paste or peanut butter

1½ tablespoons finely chopped garlic

2 teaspoons finely chopped fresh ginger

2 teaspoons chili bean sauce

3 tablespoons Chinese white vinegar or cider vinegar

2 tablespoons orange juice

2 tablespoons light soy sauce

2 teaspoons dark soy sauce

½ teaspoon salt

½ teaspoon freshly ground black pepper

2 teaspoons sugar

2 teaspoons ground roasted Sichuan peppercorns (see page 15)

1 tablespoon peanut oil

1½ tablespoons sesame oil

1 Cook the noodles in a large pan of boiling water for 3–5 minutes, then drain and plunge them in cold water.

2 Drain the noodles thoroughly and toss them with the sesame oil. Arrange them on a platter or in a large bowl.

3 The sauce can be made in advance and kept refrigerated, since it is served cold. Just mix all the ingredients together in a bowl or an electric blender.

4 When ready to serve, pour the sauce on top of the noodles and toss well, then garnish with the scallions.

Singapore noodles

This is the ultimate Fusion noodle dish. Curry is not original to Chinese cuisine. It was introduced to China centuries ago by immigrants returning home from sojourns in Southeast Asia, especially from the east coast of India. This is why even today curry continues to be popular in southern and eastern China, where many immigrants returned from faraway Singapore. Chinese cuisine readily adopts new foods and ingredients when their virtues are recognized. These light and subtle rice noodles make an ideal foil for the spicy sauce.

serves 6–8
preparation time: 20 minutes, plus 25 minutes' soaking
cooking time: 15 minutes

8 oz (225 g) thin dried rice noodles

2 eggs, beaten

1 tablespoon sesame oil

1 teaspoon salt

½ teaspoon freshly ground black pepper

3 tablespoons peanut oil

1½ tablespoons coarsely chopped garlic

1 tablespoon finely chopped fresh ginger

6 fresh red or green chilies, seeded and finely shredded

6 fresh or canned water chestnuts, peeled if fresh, sliced

2 oz (50 g) Chinese black mushrooms, soaked, stems removed (see page 11), and finely shredded

¼ lb (100 g) Chinese barbe-cue pork or cooked ham, finely shredded

3 scallions, finely shredded

4 oz (100g) cooked small shrimp, shelled

1½ cups (175 g) small, sweet frozen peas, thawed

Cilantro leaves, to garnish

For the curry sauce:

2 tablespoons light soy sauce

3 tablespoons Indian Madras curry paste or powder

2 tablespoons Shaoxing rice wine or dry sherry

1 tablespoon sugar

1 teaspoon salt

1 teaspoon freshly ground black pepper

1 cup (250 ml) canned coconut milk

¾ cup (175 ml) *Classic Chinese chicken stock* (see page 26) or good quality ready-made stock

1 Soak the rice noodles in a bowl of warm water for 25 minutes, then drain them in a colander or sieve. In a small bowl, combine the eggs with the sesame oil, salt, and pepper and set aside.

2 Heat a wok over a high heat, then add the peanut oil. When it is very hot and slightly smoking, add the garlic, ginger, and chilies and stir-fry for 30 seconds.

3 Add the water chestnuts, mushrooms, pork or ham, and scallions and stir-fry for 1 minute. Then add the rice noodles, shrimp, and peas and stir-fry for another 2 minutes.

4 Add all the sauce ingredients and cook over a high heat for 5 minutes or until most of the liquid has evaporated.

5 Now pour the egg mixture over the noodles and stir-fry constantly until the egg has set. Turn the noodles on to a large platter, garnish with cilantro leaves and serve immediately.

Menus

Here is some simple advice on how to put together a Chinese meal, plus suggested menus for a variety of occasions. Start with some of the easy ones, which will give you experience with basic cooking techniques. At first, cook just one or two Chinese dishes at a time, perhaps including them as part of a European meal. Chinese snacks, for example, make wonderful appetizers at any meal, and many Chinese dishes can successfully be combined with Western-style meats and salads.

When you prepare your first completely Chinese meal, choose two or three dishes and serve them with some plain steamed rice. Never select dishes to make that all need stir-frying or you will have a traumatic time in the kitchen trying to get everything ready at once and will arrive at the table hot and flustered. Choose instead one braised dish, a cold dish, or something that can be prepared ahead of time then warmed through, and limit your stir-frying to just one recipe. This means that not only will you gain the confidence needed to try more ambitious dishes, but also your meal will be all the more authentic for embracing a variety of techniques.

Remember that the art of Chinese cooking lies in achieving a harmonious blend of color, texture, aroma, and flavor. This involves using a range of cooking methods. A fish may be steamed, a meat braised, while the vegetables may be stir-fried. A meal will also be designed so that each dish is different and yet they all complement each other. One dish will be spicy, another mild; one may be chewy, another crisp. The total effect should appeal to all the senses. The dishes should be placed in the center of the table and shared among the diners, who help themselves and each other to a little of this and a little of that. For the Chinese, eating is a communal experience; a shared meal is regarded as the visible manifestation of the harmony that exists between family and friends.

Dinner Party for 6

This is an elegant, stylish meal for friends. It is quite ambitious but much of the work can be done ahead of time. Both the soup and the rice can be reheated. Serve the soup first, followed by the shrimp, then serve the duck and rice. Increase the quantities given in the recipes by half to serve six.

Corn and crab soup

Spicy Sichuan-style shrimp

Crispy aromatic duck

Egg fried rice

Dinner Party for 6

This is a simpler menu than the one on page 123 and is light and flavorful. Serve the fish first, followed by the chicken with spinach and rice. Increase the quantities given in the recipes by half to serve six.

Steamed Cantonese-style fish

Stir-fried chicken with black bean sauce

Stir-fried spinach

Perfect steamed rice

Dinner Party for 6

Here is a savory treat for your vegetarian friends. There is a variety of textures and tastes in this easy-to-prepare meal. Substitute vegetable stock for the chicken stock in the *Braised Sichuan-style spicy beancurd*. Increase the quantities given in the recipes by half to serve six.

Crispy "seaweed"

Stir-fried mixed vegetables

Braised Sichuan-style spicy beancurd

Perfect steamed rice

Buffet for 20

This is a very manageable feast for 20. Much of the preparation can be done hours beforehand, leaving you free to enjoy your own party. I have suggested quantities for each recipe, but this will depend on your guests' appetite!

Sesame shrimp toast
(double the recipe quantity)

Peking-style caramel walnuts
(make four times the recipe quantity)

Crispy fried wontons
(make five times the recipe quantity)

Cashew chicken
(make five times the recipe quantity)

Spring rolls
(double the recipe quantity)

Northern-style cold noodles
(make five times the recipe quantity)

Family Meal for 4

A healthy and nutritious meal
for your family.

Sweet and sour pork, Chiu Chow style

Stir-fried broccoli

Chow mein

Romantic Dinner for 2

An effortless meal that leaves time for
talking – the essence of a romantic dinner.
Serve the dishes one at a time so you can
linger over your meal. Halve the quantities
given in the recipes to serve two.

Cantonese egg flower soup

Steamed fresh oysters

Stir-fried pork with scallions

Perfect steamed rice

Index

Accompaniments 106–21
Appetizers 36–49
Asparagus
   stir-fried mixed vegetables 100–1

Bamboo brushes 20
Bean thread noodles 12
Beancurd 8
   braised Sichuan-style spicy bean
      curd 102–3
   spicy hot and sour soup 34–5
Beef
   stir-fried beef with oyster sauce
      78–9
Black bean sauce
   Cantonese crab with 62–5
   stir-fried chicken with 80–1
Black rice vinegar 17
Bok choy 8
   crispy "seaweed" 36–7
Braised Sichuan-style spicy
   beancurd 102–3
Bread
   sesame shrimp toast 38–9
Broccoli, stir-fried 98–9
Brushes, bamboo 20

Cabbage, Chinese flowering 9
Cabbage, Chinese white see Bok
   choy
Cantonese crab with black bean
   sauce 62–5
Cantonese egg flower soup 28–9
Cantonese-style fish, steamed 52–3
Cantonese wonton soup 32–3
Caramel walnuts, Peking-style 44–5
Carrots
   stir-fried mixed vegetables 100–1
   sweet and sour pork, Chiu Chow
      style 72–5
Cashew chicken 88–9
Caul fat 8
Chicken
   cashew chicken 88–9
   Chinese chicken curry 86–7
   chow mein 114–17
   classic Chinese chicken stock 26–7
   classic lemon chicken 84–5
   spicy chicken with peanuts 82–3
   stir-fried chicken with black bean
      sauce 80–1
Chili bean sauce 14
Chili dipping sauce 9
Chili oil 9
Chili powder 9
Chili sauce 14
Chilies 8–9

Singapore noodles 120–1
Chinese chicken curry 86–7
Chinese dried mushrooms 11
Chinese greens
   stir-fried mixed vegetables 100–1
Chinese leaves 10
   spring rolls 46–9
   stir-fried mixed vegetables 100–1
Chinese pancakes 106–9
Chinese tree fungus 11
Chinese wood ear fungus 12
Chopping boards 20
Chopsticks 20
Chow mein 114–17
Cilantro 10
Classic Chinese chicken stock 26–7
Classic lemon chicken 84–5
Clay pots 22
Cleavers 20
Cod
   Sichuan braised fish 54–5,
   steamed Cantonese-style fish 52–3
Conversion tables 23
Corn and crab soup 30–1
Corn on the cob
   Corn and crab soup 30–1
Corn oil 13
Cornstarch 10
Crab
   Cantonese crab with black bean
      sauce 62–5
   Corn and crab soup 30–1
Crackling Chinese roast pork 76–7
Crispy aromatic duck 92–3
Crispy fried wontons 40–1
Crispy "seaweed" 36–7
Curries
   Chinese chicken curry 86–7
   Singapore noodles 120–1

Deep-fat fryers 20–2
Dim sum–style pork dumplings 42–3
Dipping sauce, sweet and sour
   40–1
Duck
   crispy aromatic duck 92–3
   Peking duck 90–1
Dumplings, dim sum-style pork 42–3

Egg noodles 12
Eggs
   Cantonese egg flower soup 28–9
   egg-fried rice 112
   egg white 10
Equipment 19–22

Fish 50–5

Sichuan braised fish 54–5
   steamed Cantonese-style fish 52–3
Five-spice powder 10

Garlic 10–11
Ginger 11
Green beans, Sichuan-style 104–5

Halibut
   Sichuan braised fish 54–5
Ham 11
   chow mein 114–17
   dim sum-style pork dumplings 42–3
Hoisin sauce 14
Hot and sour soup 34–5

Ingredients 8–18

Lemon chicken 84–5
Lychees
   sweet and sour pork, Chiu Chow
      style 72–5

Meat 68–93
   crackling Chinese roast pork 76–7
   dim sum-style pork dumplings
      42–3
   Singapore noodles 120–1
   spring rolls 46–9
   stir-fried beef with oyster sauce
      78–9
   stir-fried pork with scallions
      70–1
   sweet and sour pork, Chiu Chow
      style 72–5
Mushrooms 11–12
   Singapore noodles 120–1
   spicy hot and sour soup 34–5

Noodles 12
   chow mein 114–17
   northern-style cold noodles 118–19
   Singapore noodles 120–1
Northern-style cold noodles 118–19

Oils 12–13
Oyster sauce 14
   stir-fried beef with oyster sauce 78–9
Oysters, steamed fresh 66–7

Pancakes, Chinese 106–9

Pastes 14–15
Peanut oil 13
Peanuts 13

spicy chicken with peanuts 82–3
Peas
    Singapore noodles 120–1
Peking cabbage see Chinese leaves
Peking duck 90–1
Peking-style caramel walnuts 44–5
Peppercorns, Sichuan see Sichuan
        peppercorns
Peppers
    Chinese chicken curry 86–7
    stir-fried squid with vegetables
        60–1
    sweet and sour pork, Chiu Chow
        style 72–5
    sweet and sour shrimp 56–7
Perfect steamed rice 110
Pine kernels
    crispy "seaweed" 36–7
Pork
    Cantonese crab with black bean
        sauce 62–5
    crackling Chinese roast pork 76–7
    crispy fried wontons 40–1
    dim sum-style pork dumplings
        42–3
    sesame shrimp toast 38–9
    Singapore noodles 120–1
    spring rolls 46–9
    stir-fried pork with scallions
        70–1
    sweet and sour pork, Chiu Chow
        style 72–5
Poultry 80–93
    cashew chicken 88–9
    Chinese chicken curry 86–7
    chow mein 114–17
    classic Chinese chicken stock
        26–7
    classic lemon chicken 84–5
    crispy aromatic duck 92–3
    Peking duck 90–1
    spicy chicken with peanuts 82–3
    stir-fried chicken with black bean
        sauce 80–1
Prosciutto
    dim sum-style pork dumplings
        42–3

Shrimp 13
    crispy fried wontons 40–1
    dim sum-style pork dumplings 42–3
    sesame shrimp toast 38–9
    Singapore noodles 120–1
    spicy Sichuan-style shrimp 58
    spring rolls 46–9
    sweet and sour shrimp 56–7

Racks, wok 20
Red rice vinegar 17
Rice 13

egg-fried rice 112
    perfect steamed rice 110
Rice cookers 22
Rice noodles 12
Rice vinegar 17
Rice wine 15

Salt 14
Salted black beans 14
Sand pots 22
Sauces 14–15
Sea bass
    Sichuan braised fish 54–5
Seasoning woks 19
"Seaweed," crispy 36–7
Sesame oil 13
Sesame paste 15
Sesame seeds 15
    Peking-style caramel walnuts 44–5
    sesame shrimp toast 38–9
Shaoxing rice wine 15
Shellfish 56–67
    Cantonese crab with black bean
        sauce 62–5
    crispy fried wontons 40–1
    sesame shrimp toast 38–9
    Singapore noodles 120–1
    spicy Sichuan-style shrimp 58
    spring rolls 46–9
    steamed fresh oysters 66–7
    stir-fried squid with vegetables 60–1
    sweet and sour shrimp 56–7
    corn and crab soup 30–1
Sherry 15
Sichuan braised fish 54–5
Sichuan peppercorns 15–17
Sichuan-style green beans 104–5
Sichuan-style shrimp 58
Sichuan-style spicy beancurd 102–3
Singapore noodles 120–1
Snowpeas 11
    chow mein 114–17
    stir-fried squid with vegetables
        60–1
Sole
    steamed Cantonese-style fish 52–3
Soups 24–35
    Cantonese egg flower soup 28–9
    Cantonese wonton soup 32–3
    spicy hot and sour soup 34–5
    corn and crab soup 30–1
Soy sauce 15
Spatulas 20
Spicy chicken with peanuts 82–3
Spicy hot and sour soup 34–5
Spicy Sichuan-style shrimp 58
Spinach 17
    stir-fried spinach 96
scallions 17
    stir-fried pork with scallions

70–1
    sweet and sour shrimp 56–7
Spring roll skins 17
Spring rolls 46–9
Squid, stir-fried with vegetables 60–1
Stands, wok 20
Star anise 17

Steamed Cantonese-style fish 52–3
Steamed fresh oysters 66–7
Steamers 22
Stir-fried beef with oyster sauce
    78–9
Stir-fried broccoli 98–9
Stir-fried chicken with black bean
    sauce 80–1
Stir-fried mixed vegetables 100–1
Stir-fried pork with scallions
    70–1
Stir-fried spinach 96
Stir-fried squid with vegetables 60–1
Stir-frying 19–20
Stock, classic Chinese chicken 26–7
Straw mushrooms 12
Sugar 17
Sweet and sour dipping sauce 40–1
Sweet and sour pork, Chiu Chow
    style 72–5
Sweet and sour shrimp 56–7

Toast, sesame shrimp 38–9
Tofu see Beancurd
Turbot
    steamed Cantonese-style fish
        52–3

Vegetables 94–105
    stir-fried mixed vegetables 100–1
Vinegars 17

Walnuts, Peking-style caramel 44–5
Water chestnuts 17–18
    dim sum-style pork dumplings
        42–3
    sesame shrimp toast 38–9
    Singapore noodles 120–1
    sweet and sour pork, Chiu Chow
        style 72–5
    sweet and sour shrimp 56–7
Wheat noodles 12
White rice vinegar 17
Woks 19–20
Wonton skins 18
    Cantonese wonton soup 32–3
    crispy fried wontons 40–1

Yellow bean sauce 15